BON
Its Encounter with Buddhism in Tibet

B.L. BANSAL

EASTERN BOOK LINKERS

DELHI INDIA

Publishers :

EASTERN BOOK LINKERS

5825, New Chandrawal, Jawahar Nagar,

Delhi-110007 Ph.: 2520287

First Edition : 1994

ISBN : 81-86339-03-5

Price EASTERN BOOK LINKERS EBL RS. 350/2

PRINTED BY: Roshan Offset Printers, DELHI

Foreword

Not many people understand the real position of Bon in the history of Tibetan religion. Mr Bansal has tried in this work to shed light on this problem.

According to Buddhism the eradication of ignorance and other evils enables one to understand the real nature of phenomena in the same way that water is purified by a fruit known as katak. The mere sound "katak" cannot purify water. A knowledge of religion by itself,i.e. without practice, can lead us nowhere. One should, therefore, purify oneself and accumulate *prajñā* or true knowledge by following the path that leads to nirvānā. The author shows that Bon as a religion and way of life points to a similar path and that the Bon tradition runs parallel to that of Buddhism.

I am quite satisfied with this work which the author has written after his retirement from Government service. To have written a work of this kind at his age definitely reflects his thirst for knowledge. It is hoped that this work will help the readers in understanding Bon and its relationship with Buddhism clearly. Furthermore, it is gratifying to note that the author is continuing his researches in the field. I wish him success and godspeed.

Geshe Gelek Gyatso

Preface

Tibet, Roof of the World, a high plateau with the highest altitudes, is a land of austere beauty continually battered by furious storms of wind, rain, hail, snow, and dust mixed with gravel. Yet, or perhaps because of it , Tibet has a unique religious culture given to it by two living traditions---Buddhism and a faith known as *Bon.* Ever since its entry into Tibet between the fifth and seventh centuries A.D. Buddhism has been the dominant religion of Tibet. *Bon* is less well known in spite of its being the native religion. Tradition characterizes it in unfavourable terms as a perversion of Buddhism. Indeed it is regarded as a religion in which Buddhist doctrines and practices have been either copied or perverted and distorted. Often it is even compared to *Shamanism.* Thanks to recent researches, however, a more accurate understanding of *Bon* has now emerged. It is recognized as closely related to the various Buddhist schools in Tibet in spite of its having an identity of its own.

This is by no means an exhaustive work on the subject, Many questions remain unanswered. The first and foremost is about the origins of *Bon.* Is *Bon* native to Tibet, or has it come from outside,and from where ? Is it only a faith or a religion? What is its contribution to the present culture of Tibet? The primary difficulty in the way of our finding answers to these quetions is the non-availability of any literature on the subject pretaining to the period before the seventh century A.D. Tibet was then without a literary language of its own. A good deal of the material relating to the subsequent centuries is of doubtful authenticity. Indeed it is based on inferences drawn from the literature of organized tradition. Further, most of the works on *Bon* are as yet untranslated from

Tibetan. The number of works that have been translated by Western Tibetologists is small. Of course they do throw considerable light on the development of *Bon* from a cult of nature worship to an organized tradition , but they only whet the appetite for more information. Meanwhile the Tibetans have had to leave the land of their birth and settle down elsewhere, mostly in India and Nepal. In India they have established a big monastery at Dharamśala in Himachal Pradesh (known as Little Tibet). a *Bon* monastic center at Dolanji, Solan and a couple of other monasteries in Karnataka in South India. Many of them have brought their scriptures with them---their precious possessions. A library of Tibetan works and archives has been established at Dharamśala. and the work of translating important documents has started. It is expected that more and more documents would become avilable and that we would soon be enabled to know more about Tibet's religious culture and attain a fuller understanding.

Neither *Bon* nor Buddhism can be studied in isolation in the context of Tibet. The account of Bon in this study, therefore, runs parallel to that of Buddhism in Tibet. In putting my facts together I have drawn on a number of pioneering works by Western Tibetologists. I have acknowledged my use of their material in the notes appended to each chapter. The bibliography at the end of the study lists some more important works. It is a select (and by no means exhaustive) bibliography. Each of the works listed there is significant and adds an important dimension to our understanding of Bon.

The idea of researching into *Bon* was first suggested to me by a scholar who is also a *Bonpo*---Mr Thupten K.Rikey. He also provided me with a good deal of material. He was kind enough to launch me on the subject and to give me useful advice from time to time. I was encouraged to undertake the work by the graciousness of Dr G.G. Gyatso of the Department of Buddhist Studies, University of Delhi. He took me in hand and guided me step by step in this new world of Tibetan religious doctrines and practice. Without him there was no question of my making this study so fruitful, so worth-while My association with Dr Gyatso was in line with the well-known guru-śiṣya tradition that has been unique to India's intellectual world. Mr A.S. Hebbar of the Jawaharlal Nehru University went through the entire draft and helped in finalizing the text. He calls his work a labour of love,and says that it celebrates our long friendship of nearly a quarter of a century. My grateful thanks are due to all those who have had a hand in the making of this study, but I shall be failling in my duty if I do not mention Professor Sanghsen Singh and Mr V.K. Singh of the department of Buddhist Studies and professor Dalip Singh Duggal, formerly Head of the Department of African Studies, University of Delhi, for their constant and loving encouragement. Professor S.K. Pathak of Santiniketan looked through the entire manuscript and suggested inclusion of some information on the traces that we can still see of *Bon* in the Northwest Himalaya. Acting on this suggestion I have provided in an appendix whatever information I could gather from published sources. I am grateful to Professor Pathak for this suggestion and generally for his interest in my work.

My wife Santosh and son Sumit stood by me during the period of study. To say that I thank them is a mere formality. My debt to them stands. I can only acknowledge it here.

B.L. Bansal

and to give me useful advice from time to time. I was encouraged to undertake the work by the graciousness of Dr G.G. Gyatso of the Department of Buddhist Studies, University of Delhi. He took me in hand and guided me step by step in this new world of Tibetan religious doctrines and practice. Without him there was no question of my making this study so fruitful, so worth-while. My association with Dr Gyatso was in line with the well-known guru-śiṣya tradition that has been unique to India's intellectual world. Mr A.S. Hebbar of the Jawaharlal Nehru University went through the entire draft and helped in finalizing the text. He calls his work a labour of love and says that it celebrates our long friendship of nearly a quarter of a century. My grateful thanks are due to all those who have had a hand in the making of this study, but I shall be failing in my duty if I do not mention Professor Sanghsen Singh and Mr V.K. Singh of the department of Buddhist Studies and professor Dalip Singh Duggal, formerly Head of the Department of African Studies, University of Delhi, for their constant and loving encouragement. Professor S.K. Pathak of Santiniketan looked through the entire manuscript and suggested inclusion of some information on the traces that we can still see of Bon in the Northwest Himalaya. Acting on this suggestion I have provided in an appendix whatever information I could gather from published sources. I am grateful to Professor Pathak for this suggestion and generally for his interest in my work.

My wife Santosh and son Sumit stood by me during the period of study. To say that I thank them is a mere formality. My debt to them stands. I can only acknowledge it here.

B.I. Pandit

Contents

CHAPTER ONE

Introduction

Bon is the primitive native religion of Tibet, and it has, in spite of the influence of Buddhism, preserved itself till the present day, albeit not in its original form. Bon monasteries and *Bon* shrines are to be found throughout Tibet, especially in East Tibet and in the western border areas of the country such as Mustang and Dolpo, which belong politically to Nepal but culturally and linguistically to Tibet[1]. Buddhism on the other hand is a foreign religion, having been introduced from India between the fifth and seventh centuries A.D., if not earlier, via Nepal, travelling along the trade routes in West and Central Asia. Its entry into Tibet was facilitated by the country's political contacts with those areas in the region where it had flourishing centres. It is at present (it was at least till A.D. 1959) the dominant religion of Tibet, with the Dalai Lama as its head.

Bon was originally a cult of nature worship. It is said to have been widespread in inner Asia, China, East and West Turkestan, Manchuria, Mongolia, and the Tibetan plateau[2]. Tibetans of the early days were apparently completely subject to their formidable natural

1. Giuseppe Tucci, *Religions of Tibet* (New Delhi, 1980), p.213.
2. Helmut Hoffman, *The Religions of Tibet*, Edward Fitzgerald, trans. (London, 1961), edn 2, p.15.

surroundings. Their religious ideas, which were rooted in and dominated by nature, revolved round the various good and evil spirits with which they peopled their wild, highland landscape. These spirits in time became gods who had to be propitiated to avert harm and worshipped to secure help. The belief in the spirits developed into a cult with its own elaborate ritual. There were *Shamans* or specialist priests who professed to be experts in controlling nature through their knowledge of the ways of propitiating the spirits. These practices varied from place to place and from clan to clan as Tibet in those days was not a unified state and was divided into a number of regions controlled by different tribes. This religion of Tibet underwent much evolution in the process of competing with the incomparably more solid doctrinal structure of Buddhism. It would seem that the teaching of *Bon* began to take on a literary form almost at the same time that Buddhism started penetrating into Tibet. The original *Bon* rites were aimed essentially at assuring protection and assistance to the person of the king who was considered to be of divine origin, as well as to the tribal chieftains and certain privileged families against evil, in situations of crisis and in the face of danger to life. The ancient Tibetan customs provided the basis for the doctrinal superstructure that was gradually constructed. This took place under the influence not only of Buddhism but also of other religious concepts and doctrines. The Tibetans owed their knowledge of these concepts to their Central Asian conquests and to their contacts with India and China.[3]

When .Buddhism reached Tibet about the seventh century A.D., it had undergone a profound change. As

3. Tucci,n.1,p.214.

taught by Sākyamuni Gautama Buddha in the sixth century B.C. it was a special way of life laid down by the Master for gentle ascetics and for men and, later, women who forsook their normal responsibilities for the homeless life of mendicants to end misery and suffering in the world and to attain salvation. It enjoined its followers to spread the word of the Buddha among the people they came in contact with. By their self-discipline and kindly demeanour, the followers of the Buddha were able to win the support of large classes of people, including the wealthy merchant class. They received lands and buildings as gifts which they used first as fixed retreats for the three months of the monsoon but which became in course of time the permanent headquarters of the self- constituted order of monks. These retreats were known as monasteries and were great seats of learning and philosophical debate, attracting students and travellers from all over the world.

By the beginning of the Christian era a vast literature began to develop not just on the teaching of the Buddha and the rules of the order established by Him but also on vast philosophical problems. These problems appeared to be more and more complex as the Buddhists came into contact with other philosophical schools and had to restate their fundamental philosophical position in the accepted idiom. A large change came about in Buddhist philosophy and ethics when different Buddhist schools emerged and sought to reinterpret the teaching of the Master. From the goal of individual salvation Buddhism moved to one of seeking salvation of all sentient beings based on the unity of wisdom and universal compassion, the essence of the Buddha's enlightenment. Then came the doctrine of universal emptiness, which held that the elements themselves were as empty of ultimate significance as the physical entities of which they formed part. This was known as the *Prajñāpāramitā* (Perfection of Wisdom) doctrine. Then there was the *Vajrayāna* doctrine, which said that it was not necessary to undergo hardship for several lives to attain salvation and that it was possible within one's own life-time by reciting certain *mantras* and establishing personal contact with divinities conceived of as beings of power armed with spiritual grace to transfer their devotees to the higher sphere of extra-sensory experience. New forms of Buddhist literature known as *tantras* came into being where various sets of divinities were described and praised, the rituals were referred to, and the state of supreme bliss that might be experienced was extolled. At this stage entered the erotic element in *Vajrayāna:* controlled use of the sexual processes was found effective in the realization of a kind of transcendental bliss that was identified with enlightenment. One offshoot of the entry of this erotic element was the acceptance of pairs of gods and goddesses.

A brief mention of the formation of different schools of Buddhism should be in order here. After His *Mahāparinirvāṇa* the teaching of the Buddha gave rise to a great divergence of views among His followers. Buddhist tradition speaks of several schools which arose in response to different situations. The number of schools that arose in India itself was as many as eighteen. We can only mention the most important among them here, i.e. those which are regarded as particularly significant to Indian thought. The divergent views could be broadly classified under two heads, *Hīnayāna* (the Small Vehicle) and *Mahāyāna* (the Great Vehicle). The word "*Hīna*" suggests that the names were devised most likely by the followers of *Mahāyāna*. Apparently *Hīnayāna* had an earlier origin. Apart from chronology there are wide differences between the two in their philosophic and ethical outlook. For instance, the followers of *Hīnayāna* believe in the reality of outward objects (and hence described in Hindu works as *Sarvāstivādins*) whereas the adherents of *Mahāyāna* adopt the opposite view. *Hīnayāa* is content to stop at pointing out the means by which an individual may release himself from the bondage of *saṁsāra*, whereas *Mahāyāna* teaches that the awakened individual should work continually for the spiritual welfare of the world. The exponents of *Mahāyāna* hold that their doctrine represents the true teaching of the Buddha and that the variations found in the *Hīnayāna* school are due either to an attempt on the part of the Master to adjust the teaching to less qualified disciples or to the inability of the latter to grasp its complete significance. Whatever the truth, it is difficult to take either as representing exactly the teaching as it was originally imparted.[4]

As has been mentioned earlier, Buddhism gradually assumed a more and more scholastic character. At the same time it never ceased to be a popular creed. By the beginning of the Christian era a large amount of literature began to appear. It is difficult to go into this vast accumulated treasure. We shall, therefore, confine ourselves to the four important schools that came into being during the period: *Vaibhāṣika*, *Sautrāntika*, *Yogācāra*, and *Mādhyamika*.

Vaibhāṣika is associated with the names of Diṅnāga and Dharmakirti (circa A.D.500). *Vibhāṣā* is the commentary on the *Abhidharma* books, and the *Vaibhāṣikas* are so called because they accept this commentary as most authoritative and final. The

4. M. Hiriyanna, *An Outline of Indian Philosophy* (London. 1967), p.197.

Sautrāntika school founded by Kumāralabdha (A.D.200) holds that, being a human composition, *Vibhāṣā* is liable to contain error. They maintain that the Buddha taught the *Abhidharma* doctrines in certain *sutrās* and *sautrāntas*. In line with this view they recognize their authority alone. Hence their name "*Sautrāntikas*". The *Vaibhāṣikas* hold that objects are directly perceived. The Sautrāntikas say that they are known indirectly inasmuch as, according to them, the same objects cannot be present at the time they are perceived. If things are really momentary, it is only a past thing that can be perceived. The realism of the *Vaibhāṣika*, as that of the *Sautrāntika*, does not indicate the being of anything except *svalakṣaṇas*. However, while one admits that a svalakṣana is directly cognized, the other views it as something that is known indirectly. Both endow the perceiving mind with a constructive side on account of which reality becomes vastly transformed when it is perceived. According to these two schools, knowledge is true so far as *svalakṣaṇa* is concerned and is false in respect of the conceptual elements involved in it.[5]

The third important school of Buddhism is called the *Yogācāra* school. The chief teachers of this school are Asaṅga and Vasubandhu, who flourished in the third century A.D. According to this school, knowledge is the sole truth and its whole content is false. There is neither subject nor object but only a succession of ideas. The stimulus always comes from within, never from without. The ideas signify nothing but themselves. A believer in *Yogacara* is, therefore, designated a *Vijñānavādin*.

The fourth school is known as *Mādhyamika*. This is associated with the name of one of the greatest

5. Ibid., pp.202-4.

philosophers that India has produced, viz. Nāgārjuna (about the second or third century A.D.). According to this school, all knowledge, whether perceptual or inferential, is relative, and there is none that is absolutely true. The school accordingly believes neither in the inner reality nor in the outer. The doctrine is, therefore, described as *Śūnyavāda*.

It was during this long period, when the above-mentioned changes and developments were taking place, that Buddhism became the religion of the greater part of Asia. It had already reached China in the first century A.D. From China it travelled to Korea and Japan. It also passed from India and Sri Lanka to Myanmar (Burma), Thailand, and Indochina and to the islands of Southeast Asia. Being a close neighbour, Nepal received in full force the developments in Indian Buddhism in its earlier as well as later forms by the fifth century A.D. Tibet inherited the Indian and Nepalese traditions a little later.[6]

Buddhism was first established in Tibet, albeit on a small scale, during the reign of the mighty monarch, King Srong brtsan sgam po, in the seventh century A.D. It would appear that the Tibetans were aware of the existence of Buddhism even in earlier times. According to one tradition, in the reign of King lHa tho thori the fourth predecessor of Srong brtsan sgam po, certain religious books fell from the sky down to the roof of his palace, but no one could understand them. These books were, therefore, kept in a separate room and worshipped in the belief that they had come from heaven. What must have happened was that some itinerant Buddhist

---

6. David L.Snellgrove and Hugh Richardson, *A Cultural History of Tibet* (Boulder, Colo., 1980), p.71.

monks travelled from Nepal to Tibet, carrying a few books with them which were quite incomprehensible in that country. Probably later they came away leaving the books behind.

During the reign of Srong brtsan sgam po, Buddhism was restricted to the court. It was inclined to compromise with *Bon*, the older faith, and come to terms with it in the interest of peaceful coexistence. *Bon,* though introduced into the country by gShen rab mi bo according to a *Bon po* tradition, had already adopted certain foreign elements. It was now exposed directly to Buddhist influence through Tibeten conquests of Central Asia. It was attracted especially by the Indian theories of *karma* and rebirth and absorbed them without acknowledging the source.[7] At this stage it was a blend of several elements - belief in the divine nature of kings, worship of associated gods, Iranian ideas on the formation of the world, and sophisticated Indian therories such as *karma* and rebirth.

In the early stages of its entry into Tibet Buddhism was cautious and conciliatory. Its adherents obtained the permission and protection of King Srong brtsan sgam po to practise their religion. Royal patronage was forthcoming for Buddhism on account of its political potential in the face of rivalries between different groups of nobles who were also ministers. Buddhism also served as a humanizing force for an otherwise rough and warlike people. According to contemporary evidence, it was, in those early days, content to compromise and to come to terms with the older faith. Indeed it sought for peaceful coexistence. It was able to exploit such common ground as there was between some of the more worldly *tantric*

7. Samten G.Karmay, *A General Introduction to the History and Doctrines of Bon* (Tokyo, 1975), p.181.

rites (as, for example, the rites for prosperity, for the destruction of enemies, etc.) and certain indigenous pre-Buddhist practices performed by priests known as *Bon* and *gShen*. This appears to have been the main achievement of Padmasambhava, the great Indian saint who established himself as a highly venerated *yogi* in Tibet.

Bon for its part, though supported by aristocrats and nobles at the court, had to struggle for its very survival in the face of the challenge from Buddhism. There were conflicts, and it is said that there was even persecution of the *Bon po* by the Royal guards. So much so that some adherents of *Bon* became Buddhists; many were expelled or went into exile following humiliating treatment. The more intelligent among the *Bon po,* however, adopted modes of operation through which they were able to enrich their discipline without jeopardizing their original identity. This may well be termed reconciliation or compromise with Buddhism made by the *Bon po* to escape social discrimination and persecution at the hands of the Buddhists.

Indian Buddhism during the eight century and after provided Tibetan Buddhism with a host of gods of varying characteristics. The *Bon po* found that they could not use the same names for their gods as the Buddhists without losing their identity. They, therefore, conceived of a hierarchy of gods corresponding to the Buddhist ones, but with new names. They even invented a future Buddha on the lines of the Buddha Maitreya but under a different garb. They absorbed all that they possibly could of Buddhist theory and practice. They developed their doctrines on the pattern of the Buddhist theology but adapted them to *Bon po* terminology. The Buddhists too on their part adopted all local beliefs that the people were interested in. Thus a great many indigenous Tibetan divinities made their way into the Tibetan Buddhist pantheon. This process of borrowing and adaptation went on for several centuries.[8]

In ancient times *Bon* had no monastic system like Buddhism. All ceremonies were performed out in the open most of the time. *Bon* religious centres were confined to the houses or tents of the priests. With the coming of Buddhism, however, the *Bon po* thought it expedient to develop an organized religious life with temples and monasteries of their own. For instance, they started using *thang kas* (painted scrolls). The forms given to *Bon po* divinities on these *thang kas* were but variations of comparable Buddhist themes. By the fourteenth century the *Bon po* organized their teaching in terms of Nine Ways. These followed from an orderly arrangement of the various religious practices, both pre-Buddhist and Buddhist, known in Tibet at that time. This work of synthesis provided a convenient summary of the entire gamut of Tibetan religious thought. The *Bon po* claimed a historical founder in gShen rab mi bo, whose life was patterned on that of the Buddha. Simultaneously they set to work on a recognized form of teaching for their own use on the basis of material already available and taking whatever suited their argument and purpose from Buddhist literature.[9]

During the period when these religious systems were thus organizing themselves, their relations were very close at the personal level. They were all competing for the interest and support of the same villagers and nomads. The lay folk were free to invite whomsoever they pleased

8. Snellgrove and Richardson,n. 6, p.107.
9. Ibid.

to perform their ceremonies. So much so that sometimes a celibate Buddhist teacher, a *tantric yogī*,and a *Bon po* were all invited together. The hostility or rivalry today between the Buddhists and the *Bon po* stems from their not realizing the extent of the amalgamation that the two religions have undergone. Indeed they both use the term "*Sangs rgyas*" (amply purified) for a perfected sage or a Buddha. By accepting so many Buddhist forms, rites, and observances and by allowing so many *Bon* practices to be incorporated into Tibetan Buddhism the *Bon po* have achieved the status of *nang pa* or insiders.

However, this amalgamation of doctrine and religious practice notwithstanding, there obtains a fundamental difference between the Buddhists and the *Bon po*. All Buddhists acknowledge the Indian origin of their doctrine and continue to hold the historic Buddha, or Śākyamuni, in deepest reverence. The *Bon po* on the other hand persist in their claim that the very same Buddhist teaching came from a country called sTag gzigs (Iran in a vague sense) and that the original Buddha was gShen rab mi bo, not Śākyamuni. None the less the *Bon po*, exactly like the Buddhists, perform ritual acts as prescribed by their religion with the pious intention of eventually becoming "awakened" and with unquestioning faith in their Buddha so that in this sense they may be considered to be as profoundly Buddhist as any others. (That the Buddha in their view is gShen rab mi bo is another matter.) Certainly their monks (who are strictly celibate) consider themselves "sons of the Buddha" - in the perspective of their own tradition.

The advent of Buddhism coincided with or was the occasion for the adoption of a system of writing for the first time in Tibet. The keeping of records soon followed. The circumstances, the history, and the form in which

Buddhism came to Tibet are, therefore, well documented although Buddhism is not native to Tibet. On the other hand there is little definite information concerning the pre-Buddhist religion of Tibet. No writing is known to have existed in the land at that time, and there are no indigenous records. The pre-Buddhist religious system in Tibet is thus fogged by myth and legend.

There is another problem regarding the early Tibetan religious system. The beliefs and practices of *Bon* as we find them at present are significantly different from those that obtained before Buddhism was introduced into Tibet. *Bon* has undergone far- reaching changes in the wake of the adoption of Buddhist doctrines even as Buddhism has been transformed with the adoption of local divinities and *Bon* practices. However, there is evidence to suggest that the early religion of Tibet was not a unified system. In any case it was not unified and organized till a relatively late date from a loose aggregate of regional or tribal cults which were sufficiently non-antagonistic to coexist and to lend themselves to syncretism.[10]

Western scholars have been deeply interested in the study of the various aspects of Tibetan life, history, culture, and religion and its mysteries for long and especially since the Chinese takeover in 1950-51. For the study of the early history, religion, and other aspects of Tibet they have utilized the following principal sources of data : (a) The *Bon* religion as it obtains today, *Bon* scriptures, doctrines, rituals, iconography, sculpture, shrines, monasteries and other monuments, etc.; (b) Tibetan Buddhism with special reference to those traits and practices which are manifestly foreign to Buddhism; (c) Tibetan religious writings or Tibetan religious history;

10. Robert B.Ekval, *Religious Observances in Tibet* (Chicago, III., 1964), p.17.

(d) Tibetan historical writings together with folklore and epic works; (e) Chinese historical records which deal with Tibet, especially Tun- huang documents; and (f) religious practices of neighbouring people such as the Mongols, the Chinese, the Chiang, and the Nepalese, particulary those living in the area of Mustang and Dolpo. These are of particular importance whenever links of affinity or association seem probable.

The present study is an attempt to analyse the practices of the *Bon* religion and of Buddhism in Tibet, their historical developement, and their adaptation of each other's doctrines and religious practices and to show that the two religions, as at present constituted, shade into each other, so that the systematized *Bon* that has evolved since the introduction of Buddhism into Tibet may very well be called a tradition of Tibetan Buddhism. *Bon* is akin to *rNying ma pa,* the old sect of Buddhism in Tibet, in doctrine and ritual. According to Sarat Chandra Das, "theories and notions of the *Bon* bear striking resemblance to those of the *rDzogs chen pa* sect of the *rNying ma pa* school".[11] The present study is not intended to be either a history of *Bon* or a history of the introduction of Buddhism into Tibet. It indicates or analyses events in the history of both to the extent necessary to explain growth in their doctrines or religious practices and observances. It also tries to delineate the similarities and differences in the practices and beliefs of the two religions, which may at first sight appear to be the same. It thus shows how, barring the controversy about the foreign origins of *Bon* and the pretensions of the different founders, *Bon* is now a systematized sect of Buddhism in Tibet.

---

11. Cited in J.F.Rock, *The Na-Khi Naga Cult and Related Ceremonies,* Part I (Rome, 1952), p.7.

CHAPTER TWO

Physical Features and Early History of Tibet

Physical Features

Tibet, Land of Snow, is a fascinating country, especially to an outsider. It is also a forbidden land being fortified as it were by snowclad mountains. Therein lie its mysteries. In ancient times it was called "Bod", a word derived from "Bon" and denoting the early religion of Tibet. Those living along the Indo-Tibetan Borders refer to the Tibetans as Bhotias, a name derived from the Sanskrit word "Bhoṭa". The word "Tibet" is derived from the Mongolian "Thubet". It is known as "Tufan" in China, as "Thibet" in Thailand, and as "Tubhat" among the Arabs. It is also referred to as "Khawachen" or "Gangjong", meaning the abode of snow, and as "Sildanjong", meaning the land with a cool climate.[1]

Tibet has massive mountains on the south, west, and north, ranging in height from six to eight thousand metres above sea level along the Himalaya and the Karakoram, and from five to seven thousand metres along the Kun lun range. It is almost inaccessible. There is no well-defined mountain barrier on the east, but the vast

---

1. Tsepon W.D. Shakabpa, *Tibet: A Political History* (London/New Haven, Conn.,1967), p.l.

uninhabited wastes and a whole series of subsidiary mountain ranges keep the centre of Tibetan civilization cut off from the rest of the world. The general level of West and Central Tibet is from four to five thousand metres above sea level, and the whole country is traversed by subsidiary mountain ranges which rise to six thousand metres or more. The central part of the country lies on either side of the axis formed by the great river *gTsang po* (known in India as the Brahmaputra), which arises near *Ti se* (Mount Kailāsa) and the lake *Ma pham* (Mānsarovar) and flows eastwards along the whole southern length of the country and then south-west-wards through Assam in India to join the Bay of Bengal. Its source lies close to those of two other major rivers, the Indus and the Sutlej, which flow in the opposite direction, i.e. from the east to the west, and then turn south. On the northeast flow the mighty rivers, the *Salween*, the *Mekong*, and the *Kinsha Kiang* (known in China as the Yang-tse), from the north to the south, with high mountain ranges keeping them apart.[2]

About three-sevenths of Tibet constituting its northern part is a virtually uninhabited wilderness of mountain spurs and ranges, interspersed with black barren plains and numerous pools and lakes of brackish water. It is an area of intense cold and bitter winds and short spells of heat. Here live wild yaks (*drong*), asses (*rkyang*), and antelopes (*gstod*), as also the wolves that prey upon them. Rarely do hunters visit these regions, but the area was traversed by several adventurous foreign travellers in the late nineteenth and early twentieth centuries. Another two- sevenths of the country, again high and cold, is a rolling plateau of lofty ranges of snowcapped mountains

2. R.A.Stein, *Tibetan Civilization* (London, 1972), p.20.

and great lakes. The region is inhabited by nomadic groups of men and their large herds of yaks, sheep, and goats. The rest of the country comprises the extensive valleys of the *gTsang po* and the *Salween*, the *Mekong* and the *Kinsha Kiang*. As these areas contain the only favourable agricultural lands in the whole country, it is here that much of the sparse population of Tibet (estimated at three- and-a-half to four million) is concentrated. They contain many scattered villages and a few towns peopled by traders, officials, and the landed gentry. They also have a number of temples, monasteries, and nunneries of different religious orders.[3]

This threefold division of Tibet into valley lands, pasture lands, and wastes does not include the extreme western areas which drain into the upper waters of the Indus and the Sutlej, and a few low lying fertile valleys bordering Nepal. If one forgets the political frontiers, Tibetan culture extends to the regions of Ladakh and Lahaul and Spiti which are now under Indian administration, to Dolpo and Mustang which form part of Western Nepal, and to Sikkim and Bhutan. Sikkim is now a part of the Indian Union; Bhutan is an independent country.[4]

The two basic ways of life in Tibet are the agricultural and the nomadic. The two are in fact complementary to each other. The products of herdsmen such as meat, butter, cheese, and wool are exchanged for grain. In the intermidiate areas there are those who practise both agriculture and animal husbandry. Almost all Tibetans, like herdsmen everywhere else, keep animals

3. David L.Snellgrove and Hugh E.Richardson, *A Cultural History of Tibet* (Boulder, Colo.,1980), pp.19-21.
4. Ibid.

of some kind or other. Nomads who live nearest to the farm lands are familiar with the ways and habits of settled communities. The majority of the people live in the southern valleys and pasture lands. With their simple basic requirements the Tibetans have achieved higher standards of living than elsewhere in Asia, but severe conditions of travel have isolated them from the surrounding cultures.[5]

The Area

Tibet is a vast land with a population sparsely spread over the high plateau. There is very little human activity except in the valleys. It is more than fifteen hundred miles from the borders of China on the east to the borders of Kashmir on the west. From the north to the south the width varies from six to eight hundred miles. This distance would appear to be all the greater if viewed in the light of the topography of Tibet and the primitive means of travel its people employ. Much of the country is high terrain where only sturdy people can go. High mountain passes, deep gorges, unbridged rivers, and great plains which are either waterless deserts or vast bogs are common features of the country. The difficulty of negotiating long distances in the harsh conditions of the country causes the people to live in small isolated communities. Individuals too are particularly alone on the mountains as they go about their concerns. The common Tibetan is much on his own. He knows, solitude; for he and his fellows are spread so thinly across the bleak, austere landscape.[6]

---

5. Ibid.
6. Robert B.Ekval, *Religious Observances in Tibet* (Chicago,III., 1964), p.6.

The Climate

The climate of Tibet is characterized by extremes of temperature, precipitation, and wind. Over much of the plateau an average diurnal range of 50^0 to 60^0 F. of temperature is general throughout the year. In summer it varies from near or below freezing-point at night to 80^0-90^0 F. in the middle of the day. In winter the temperature varies from - 20^0 F. or lower to 40^0 F. In rapid succession the Tibetan experiences extremes of frost, burning sunshine, and storms of rain, pelting hail, and driving snow. Such constant and extreme variations in temperature must have a peculiar effect on the psyche and physical conditions of the people in Tibet.[7] It is, however, difficult to tell.

Similarly there are extreme variations in precipitation. The eastern and northern areas receive more rain and snow than the western and southern parts of the country. Over most of the area, precipitation is heaviest from April to October. Thus the eastern and northern areas may be little more than a bog in summer time, but in winter not only are they frozen, but the ice dries up and finding water for livestock becomes a problem. The snows are carried off by extremely strong winds and get mixed up with dust and gravel. Frequent hailstorms in summer all over Tibet constitute a special danger. Not only do they destroy the crops altogether, but they cause extensive loss of life in the case of nomads. Furthermore, the winds are of unbelievable intensity and duration, in particular throughout the winter and in early spring. Clouds of dust and storms of gravel and good-sized pebbles sweep the open plateau and literally drive everything before them. It is impossible to keep a caravan moving

7. Ibid.

head-on against such a battering. Men are sometimes blown off their horses. For a part of the year, the Tibetans live in a continuous struggle with the storm, "a tireless antagonist that scours the walls of houses, pushes hard at the doors and tears at the people and the tents with savage fingers, snatching the very earth under their footsteps".[8]

The power of this combination of topography and climate on the minds of the Tibetans is difficult to convey in words. According to the Tibetans, one has to be there to feel the height, to breathe the air, to smell the scented valleys, and to experience the silence in quiet moments. But when it is tumultuous, one feels as though the world were coming to an end. There are earthquakes when the earth opens up to swallow whole villages. There are storms that can wash away whole hillsides in a matter of minutes. The noise of a wind approaching can swell and surge until there is nothing but sound all round. In these hours it seems to threaten the very existence of all things that are not a part of the wilderness.[9]

The People

The ethnic makeup of Tibet consists of different racial types living side by side. The predominant strain is Mongoloid. Some travellers have noted the prevalence of what they describe as the Red Indian type, notably in Kongpo and among the Hor nomads. Some others have noted a European, Hellenic, or Caucasian element, especially in Northeast Tibet. A dwarfish type occurs in Chala, a district of Kham. Of course all these are but

---

8. Ibid.
9. Thubten Jigme Norbu and Colin M. Turnbull, *Tibet: Its History, Religion, and People* (London, 1969), pp.119-20.

impressions, but the fact remains that different types obtain in Tibet. However, the anthropologists distinguish just two types - one distinctly Mongoloid, and of slight build, spread throughout Tibet and the other of taller build typical of Kham. Blue-eyed blond types have also been observed in the northeast. The explanation for the presence of different ethnic groups seems to be that different populations have occupied various parts of Tibet in the course of history. They remain there still.[10]

Tibet's Neighbours

In ancient times there was a small kingdom, the kingdom of Nepal, to the south of Tibet. This kingdom consisted of what is now known as the Nepal Valley, which depended upon the trade passing north and south through it. Thus there were already trading connexions between Nepal and Tibet long before the Tibetans became a recognized political Power.

To the west of Tibet was a country of vague definition known as Shang shung (also spelt Zhang Zhung). The capital of this country was *Khyung lung* which lay to the west of Mount *Ti se*. The country consisted of the whole area now known as West Tibet and possibly extended further to the east. It was probably already in contact with the neighbouring Indian regions of Kulu and Jullundhra across the same Himalayan passes that are in use today. The important thing to note here is that Mount *Ti se* and the lake *Ma pham* formed part of Shang shung which in Tibetan tradition was the home of *Bon,* the pre-Buddhist religion of Tibet. *Ti se* is sacred to Indians and a place of pilgrimage to the Hindus. This connexion between the Hindus and *Ti se* may go back to the times when Shang shung was still independent of Tibet.[11]

10. Stein, n.2, p.20.
11. Ibid.

Further west lay *Kha che* (Kashmir), *Bru sha* (Gilgit), and Baltistan. *Kha che* was renowned as a great Buddhist land.Chinese Buddhist pilgrims visited it quite often, especially from the fifth century to the eighth. On the northwest there were Khotan, Turkestan, and Kashgar. On the northeast, Tibet was in contact with the *Chiang* tribes who peopled China's northwestern borders, within reach of the Taklamakan trade routes. The routes linked China not only with India but also with Iran and ultimately with Byzantium. All kinds of cultural ideas and motifs made their way into Tibet through these ancient routes. Quite a few of them seem to have reached Tibet even in prehistoric times.[12]

Origin of Tibet

The early history of Tibet is a mystery. So far as we are concerned the history of Tibet commences with the introduction of Buddhism or of Chinese influence into that country. Perhaps all the events now chronicled as having happened prior to this period are in large measure imaginary. There was another tendency in the early historians of Tibet. When, during the reign of Ral pa can (circa A.D. 836), they started writing their national history, they stretched the genealogies of their monarchs back to the Buddha Himself or to one of His friends and close disciples. The first Tibetan monarch, according to these historians, was descended from King Prasenajit of Kosala, an early convert and a lifelong friend of Gautama Buddha.[13]

According to Tibetan tradition, their first parents were a monkey king who was sent to the snowy kingdom

12. Snellgrove and Richardson, n.3,p.27.
13. W.Woodville Rockhill, *The Life of Buddha* (Varanasi, 1972), p.205.

by Bodhisattva *Avalokiteśvara* and a female demon who was an emanation of *Tārā,* the consort of *Avalokiteśvara.* These two had six childern, and as soon as they were weaned, the father took them into a forest of fruit trees and abandoned them there. When, after a few years, he came back, he found to his great surprise that their number had increased to five hundred. They had eaten all the fruits in the forest; and, possessed by hunger, they stood around him, clamouring piteously for food. The monkey king then cried out to his patron *Avalokiteśvara* for help from tne top of the *Potala* mountain. The god, hearing him, declared that he would be the guardian of his race and cast down a large quantity of five kinds of grain. The famished apes fell upon the grain and ate to their hearts' content. What was left over sprouted and yielded enough for their future wants. The result of eating the grain was wonderful. Their tails and the hair on their bodies grew shorter and shorter until they finally disappeared. The monkeys commenced to speak. In fact they became men and women. As soon as they noticed this change in themselves, they clothed themselves with leaves. According to some sources, the land of monkeys and female demons was Amdo, northeast of Tibet; others maintain that it was the land southeast of Tibet in a mountainous area covered with forests (and inhabited even today by monkeys). These lands are comparatively warm and suitable for agriculture. The six original clans of Tibet, the descendants of the first monkey and the female demon might, therefore, be placed more or less in the region east of the country. Although the Tibetans call them their ancestors, they always describe them as wild people or non-Tibetan aboriginals.[14] According to Tibetan

14. Stein, n.2, p.28.

tradition, from their monkey ancestor the first inhabitants inherited hairy bodies and red faces, and from the female demon they derived their tail-less form and their taste for meat. Some inherited devotion, zeal, wisdom, and kindliness from their father; others acquired from their mother the lust to kill as also physical strength and courage.

The Chinese sources link the origin of the Tibetan people to the nomadic, non-Chinese *Chiang* tribes who herded sheep and cattle in East Central Asia up to the farthest northwestern borders of China many centuries before the Christian era. According to them this is clear from the extensive nature of Tibetan farming with its ever-present element of animal husbandry, from the readiness of the Tibetans to travel long distances, from their seemingly inborn ability to handle and look after horses, yaks and other animals and from their delight in open air and open spaces coupled with their sturdy individualism. The most important part of this legacy was the presence of a large number of nomads, depending entirely on their flocks of sheep and goats and their herds of yaks. These nomads were forever on the move, and, whenever they encamped, they lived in tents. They scarcely ever saw four walls in the whole of their lives except for those of small remote monasteries. Till recently they were divided into small clans which were constantly at war with one another. The Chinese considered them as an assemblage of ferocious, barbarous tribes. Each year these nomads took "a little oath" to affirm their loyalty to their chiefs (brtsan po, "noble") and sacrificed sheep, dogs and monkeys. Every three years they took "the great oath" and sacrificed men, horses, oxen, and donkeys.[15]

Literary sources suggest a continuous movement of rival clans of Tibetan-speaking people from the general complex of tribes in the far northeastern part of the country towards the more fertile valleys of Central and South Tibet, where they adopted a partly agricultural way of life and settled down about the beginning of the Christian era. Each of these clans presumably consisted of a chief with his family and hereditary retainers and bondsmen. When they settled down, the chief's family became a kind of aristocracy. A world of rival chiefs then came into existence, with their fortified strongholds in the valleys of the central and eastern tributaries of the *gTsang po*. To the north of them were areas inhabited by momadic people who now and then displaced those who had become settled. This went on till the sixth century A.D. Central Tibet then took the offensive, and the infiltrations from the northeast ceased except for occasional marriage alliances. At a particular stage of these developments some local chiefs accepted as their overlord the powerful chief who ruled the *Yar lung* Valley, building him up into a king strong enough to force his neighbours to take notice of his pre-eminence.[16]

First King

According to Tibetan tradition the first king of Tibet descended from the sky by means of a sort of ladder (*dmu*) which passed through the various atmospheric layers. There are several versions as to who he was. Some say that he was a criminal who had been exiled from India. Others say that he was Prince Rupati of the *Kaurava* clan which was defeated by the *Pāṇḍavas* in the *Mahābhārata* War and that this prince as a fugitive found

15. Rockhill, n.13, p.206.
16. Snellgrove and Richardson, n.3, p.22.

his way into Tibet. According to Sum pa mkhan po who lived in the eighteenth century A.D., the King of Vatsala, Udayana, had a son whose eyes were covered by the lower eyelids and whose brows were turquoise blue and teeth jet white and even. He had, besides, the mark of a wheel in either palm of his hands, and there were webs between his fingers. Deciding that all this boded evil, they had him put in a copper box and cast him into the *Ganga*. One day a peasant found him and looked after him. According to another version the people gave him to a hermit. Howsoever it was, the boy grew up. Not happy about the way he was regarded, he ran away to the Himalaya. Presently he arrived at the sacred mountain *Rol tse* (Enlightenment Peak) in the range *Yar lha sham po* in *Yar lung*. Twelve men who were then worshipping the local divinity, saw him *enter the brtsan thang sgo zhi* ("Four-Portaled Plain of the Mighty"). They asked him who he was and where he came from. Not understanding their language, the young man pointed to the peak of the mountain. Thinking that he had descended from the sky, the twelve men decided to make him king. They took him with them, carrying him in a palanquin on their necks. For this reason the young man was called gNya khri brtsan po[17] ("Neck-Enthroned Mighty One"). The people of Tibet at that time were all adherents of *Bon*. The twelve men who received the young man were chieftains representing different clans. They made him king after accepting him into the *Bon* faith.[18]

The first king of Tibet, having come from the sky, had a distinct sacral quality. He was known also as lHa brtsan po ("Divine Mighty One") and lHa sras ("Divine

---

17. David L.Snellgrove, *Buddhist Himalaya* (Oxford, 1957), p.127.
18. Norbu and Turnbill, n.9, p.137.

Son"). His successors too shared this sacral quality. Being sons of the gods, they are supposed to have returned to heaven by means of the sky ladder, leaving no mortal remains on the earth. In fact the first seven kings could be properly described as gods exercising earthly functions. The final return of a king to heaven was at his death which always took place when his son was thirteen and had learnt to ride a horse. The ascent was performed with the help of the sky ladder. The body dissolved into the rope of the ladder, which resembled a rainbow extending from his head to the sky. What must have actually happened was that when the son was thirteen and was able to ride a horse, the king was pressurized into withdrawing "to a ritual death". This custom was humanized later "by a ceremonial association of the heir with kingship when he reached the age of thirteen accompanied perhaps by some pressure on the king himself to withdraw from active life".[19]

This period was distinguished by the absence of earthly burial places. It ended with the tragic end of the last king named Gri gum, who was also a god in human form but filled with arrogance. Once he challenged his subjects and relations to a duel. None dared, but a man called Lo ngam, who was master of the horse, accepted the challenge. The contest took place near *Ti se*. In the struggle King Gri gum inadvertently severed the sky ladder that connected him with heaven and was killed. He thus became the first king to leave his corpse behind. The king had three sons- Sha khri, Nya khri, and Bya khri. These fled. But the queen had another son by miracle by the god *Yar lha sham po*. This son was named Ru las skyes. Ru las skyes killed the usurping Lo ngam, brought back Prince Bya khri, and enthroned him as sPu lde sku rgyal, himself becoming the first of a series of

---

19. Snellgrove and Richardson, n.3, p.28.

seven wise ministers. He retrieved the dead body of the king and arranged for its burial at Chinga takste. However, since there were no priests in Tibet acquainted with burial rites, some were sent for from *Kha che, Bru sha*, and *sTag gzigs*. This is the period in which the later tradition i.e. the tradition beginning in the fourteenth century A.D., places the rise of the *Bon* religion, which is invariably linked with foreign lands such as *sTag* gzigs or a country called *Gurnawatra* said to be situated on the borders of India and Iran.[20] However, as the priests belonging to the *Bon* religion were already there in Tibet, this period might have seen the beginnings of systematization of *Bon* and its subsequent emergence as an organized religion. But more about this later.

It would appear that the early rulers of this small Tibetan kingdom of Yar lung were little more than princelings. Their power and influence was confined to a small area, and fluctuated with their personal ability. Not until the reign of Srong brtsan sgam po did Tibet become a mighty Power ranging from the plains of India and the mountains of Nepal to the frontiers of China, including Shang shung which is now West Tibet. During the whole of the period, there were nobles belonging to different clans, including those on the ruler's mother's side, who continued to play an important part in Tibetan history for two-and-a-half centuries of Kingly power. The nobles at the time of enthronement of a king took an oath of fealty to the king in return for the king's oath of protection and maintenance of their rights. The nobles were almost kingmakers, and through the whole of the Royal period, Kingly power relied on their support for running the kingdom. Most of them acted as ministers of State. The rulers succeeded in preserving their independence by a

20. Stein, n.2, pp.49 and 281-2.

skilful manipulation of rivalries among the nobles. In this game of life and death-for most rulers died young and by violence-the maternal relations (*zhang*) were an important factor; for the protection of a young successor to the throne fell to the lot of the kinsmen of his mother. Several of the Royal mothers appear to have come from clans or tribes outside Tibet. This added a new element to the competition for first place between the clans of Tibet proper and those of maternal relations from beyond the borders. Skill in playing off one party against another does not, however, appear to be a sufficient explanation for the long viability of kingship. The key factor seems to have been the sacral quality which made the ruler a religious symbol and the sole guarantor of the unity that was essential to national strength. The Royal title "Phrul gyi lha brtsan po" ("Divine Mighty One Magically Manifest") denotes the sacral and mystical nature of the ruler. This was further emphasized by the elaborate ceremonies of burial. (All the special possessions of the ruler and, at one time, even his personal companions were buried with him in his tomb).[21]

A description of Tibetan life and manners by outsiders is to be found in the records of the Tang dynasty of China. This assessment[22] of the Tibetan people and the description reproduced below of their mode of life appear to belong to the early seventh century A.D. when King Srong brtsan sgam po, finding the ancestral capital in the Yar lung Valley too remote from the centre of the newly united nation, moved on to Lhasa, where he built a comparatively small fort on the top of the red hill *Marpo ri* that was to be the exact site of the future *Potala*.

21. Snellgrove and Richardson, n.3, p.28.
22. Ibid., pp.29-30.

We are told that the country has a very cold climate, that oats, barley, wheat, and buckwheat grow there, and that there are yaks, as also excellent sheep and dogs, horses and pigs. The capital, a walled city with houses provided with flat roofs, is called Lhasa. The king and his nobles live in tents which are joined together as one large one. They sleep in unclean places, and they never wash or comb their hair. For the most part the people lead a pastoral life with their flocks and herds without any fixed habitation. They dress in felt and leather and paint themselves with red ochre; the women plait their red hair. They worship the heavens and believe in sorcerers and soothsayers. They know little about the cycle of seasons; their year begins when barley is ripe in the fields. Their games are chess and dice; for music they have conch-shells and drums. They have no writing for official purposes, and they record agreements and other understandings arrived at by them by means of knotted cords and notched tally-sticks. They make vessels by bending around a piece of wood and fitting it in a leather bottom, or they make basins of felt. They knead roasted grain (tsam pa) into little cups, which they fill with broth or curds, and then they eat from those cups all together. They drink their beer out of their own cupped hands.

There are hundreds of thousands of men ready to bear arms. To levy troops the king's men use a golden arrow (as insignia of authority); when they want to give warning of enemy attack they start a fire and smoke signals. There is a watch-tower every hundred li. Their armour and helmets are excellent. When they put them on, their whole body is covered, with holes just for the eyes. They carry bows and swords at all times. They prize physical strength and despise old age. A mother salutes her sons. A son has precedence over his father. When they go out, the young men always go first; the older men follow after them. Their military descipline is strict. In battle it is after the troops in front have been completely wiped out that the troops behind them come up into line. They prize death in battle and hate to die of an illness. Families in which several generations have died fighting battles are considered to be of the highest rank. When someone is defeated in battle or runs away, they fix a fox-tail to his head to show that he is cowardly like the fox. A great crowd assembles, and he is put to death. They feel it a great shame to die so, and they consider it far better to die fighting in a battle.

As for punishment, they put out the eyes of a man, or cut off his feet or nose, even for a small fault. They flog him with leather whips without any fixed number of cuts. They dig the earth and make pits several feet deep, and they keep their prisoners for two or three years in the pits so made.

The king and five or six of his followers are bound in friendship: it is called "living in common". When the king dies, such followers are all killed sacrificially. His garments, his treasures, the horses he has ridden, etc. are interred, and a large chamber is made which is covered with a mound. Trees are planted around it. It is in this place that ancestral sacrifices are performed.

On the other hand the Indians regard the Himalayan snows to their north as the home of the gods and the *Vidyadharas* (*Rig 'dzin*) who are, according to them, some kind of supermen gifted with special knowledge, particularly in the understanding of magic. This belief appears to account for the occultist tradition. They look upon Tibet as the dwelling-place of the immortal sages who guard the ultimate secrets. The Tibetans, however, locate this whole geographical and religious complex in the region north of their own country, in Khotan or in Turkestan where, they believe, the mythical country of *Shambala* lies-to be approached by routes at first real, then imaginary.[23]

---

23. Stein, n.2, p.3

CHAPTER THREE

Bon Religion : Origin and Evolution

Early Religion

Alone in the face of such powers of nature as we have outlined in the previous chapter, man found that he was wholly defenceless and that the only way open to him was to submit to the forces around him. He, therefore, deified the forces of nature: he made them into gods. Mountains and rivers, rocks and springs, land and sky, and trees and bushes became the dwelling-places of those gods. They were probably not conceived of as inherently good or bad but as beings having just the power to help or to harm, to create or to destroy. The helpful ones were worshipped, and the harmful ones propitiated. The main ingredients of worship or propitiatory rites were offerings in the form of food, drink, clothing, and even stones. Man also devised certain formulae to please the gods, and he recited them in a manner he considered best suited to them. These were all a recognition of the powers beyond his control and constituted an attempt on his part to come to terms with those powers. At first people made simple offerings themselves, but some of them seemed to achieve better results than the others. Then, gradually, there arose a professional class of

Shamans or priests.[1] In due course the rites as well as the offerings and the recitations became more and more complicated. The offerings assumed various forms, including animal sacrifice, depending on the crisis to be warded off. This kind of religious life regulated all the relationships between the Tibetan people and the immense uncertain world of spirits.

The spirits appeared to assist the Tibetans in their difficulties and, when properly propitiated, to stand by them in their incessant struggle to defend themselves against obstacles and dangers and against open and secret adversaries. These adversaries threatened their existence everywhere, their well- being, and their property. Often it was perceived that the various numinous powers were themselves the cause of misfortune. The life of the Tibetans was thus enclosed, as it were, in a world of multifarious divine manifestations; all appearances were suffused with religious sugnificance.[2]

The religion of ancient Tibet had three components.[3] During the legendary period of the kings gNya khri and sPu lde sku rgyal and before that of Srong brtsan sgam po the country was protected by the *Bon po*, the story-tellers (*sGrungs*), and the singers of riddles (*lDe'u*). Of these the Bon po are better remembered. The story-tellers and the singers of riddles must have had a religious significance as their functions were regarded as running parallel to those of the *Bon po.* Between them they must have presented what is known as the religion of man (*mi*

1. Thubten Jigme Norbu and Colin M. Turnbill, *Tibet : Its History, Religion, and People* (London, 1969), p.121.
2. Giuseppe Tucci, *Religions of Tibet* (New Delhi, 1980), p.165.
3. R.A.Stein, *Tibetan Civilization* (London, 1972), pp.191-6.

chos), as distinct from the religion of the gods (*lha chos*) - a term denoting at first *Bon* and later Buddhism.

The Story-tellers

The stories and songs were supposed to protect the kingdom, like the rites of *Bon*, through their mystic power. They were considered to express the wisdom of the elders and their trustworthy nature in lending sanction to the social and world order, to the structure of the environment and to that of the group inhabiting it. To ratify a group's relationship with the gods and the ancestors, it was essential to go back during each recitation of the stories to the origin of the institution concerned, and the recitation had to be quite authentic. By conforming to the patterns and precedents laid down in the times when things originated, one took one's place in the scheme of things and helped in upholding it. The function of the story tellers in protecting the kingdom consisted in the correct recitation of the legends. It was considered a religious act necessary for upholding the world order. The stories included those relating to the origin of the different tribes and clans, the genealogies of the rulers, the myths centring on the creation, the origin of ceremonies (*bsang*), and the like. They were invariably in the form of songs.

Singers of Riddles

The singers of riddles must have had similar duties. What they sang were songs in the form of questions and answers relating to the creation of the world and human and divine genealogies. The singers practised their art during the festive races held at holy places. An important riddle was the legend of the egg. It gave a brief outline of the genealogies of the rulers and then referred to the way the various clans arose out of an agg. It said that the egg appeared at first as the quintessence of the five elements. From its outer shell was born the white rock of the gods on high; from its inner fluid was formed the white lake of the conch; and from the glutinous part in the middle arose all beings. The soft part of the egg in its turn became eighteen eggs. One (or six) of these in the middle appeared to be made of conch. It was in fact a shapeless man without limbs, and bereft of the five senses, but endowed with thought. In accordance with his wish, the organs of sense came into being, and he became a handsome young man, King Yemon or Sangs po bum khri. He had a son by a queen. After some generations the gods came down from heaven to the earth. One of these gods, 'Ode lde sku rgyal, was elsewhere regarded as the royal dynasty's great ancestor. Two generations later, with Thing ge, we come to the ancestors of the great nations and then to those of the ancient clans (including the clan of *Lang*).

Such legends made up the *Bon po* creation myth. They were strongly influenced by similar legends current in India, Iran, and China. They were like the armorial bearings of noble families, with each family claiming divine origin and trying to establish its connexions with famous ancestors. One variant of the egg legend spoke of two birds. There were eighteen eggs in their nest-six white, six yellow, and six blue. (These colours denote the colours of the three levels of the world and their deities.) From the six middle eggs came men. Then there appeared three smiths, each belonging to one of the three realms - the gods on high (*lha*, white), on the earth (*gnyan*, yellow), and under the earth (*klu*, blue). To these was added a human smith who came from the middle realm.

Bon : Definition

The Bon component of the ancient religion of Tibet, according to the earliest texts, is tied up with the legends and deities of the indigenous folk religion, but it is no easy matter to tell the one from the other. The origins of the word "*Bon*" are as yet not clear. Some Western scholars understand *Bon* as referring primarily to certain pre-Buddhist Tibetan religious practices, vaguely described as animistic or Shamanistic - as, for instance, the conjuring up of gods by means of magic formulae.[4] However, the term "*Bon*" is never used in early Tibetan literature with any such meaning. The *Bon po* were just a class of priests whose practices and beliefs were covered by the general term "*lha chos*", which means sacred conventions, as against "*mi chos*", which denotes human conventions. It is only much later that the term "*Bon*" came to signify a whole set of religious practices. Says Ekval : "It is not certain that the word "*Bon*" referred to one unified religion, for there is some evidence which suggests the possibility that the early religion of Tibet was not a unified system or at least was unified and organized at a relatively late date."[5] Another Tibetologist, Tucci, feels that "*Bon*" is a generic term and that it includes even the *gShen*.[6] The *gShen* were priests who, with the help of their assistants, officiated at sacrifices. In the period of the dynasties, there already was a religion with its own ceremonies and liturgies, with different kinds of priests specializing in various kinds of functions. The multiplicity of liturgical acts and of performers as well as of genealogies and cosmologies shows that this religion was by no means a simple matter even then. It had a mythology of its own. It had a pantheon that varied from place to

---

4. David L.Snellgrove, *Nine Ways of Bon* (Boulder, Colo., 1980), p.20.
5. Robert B.Ekval, *Religious Observances in Tibet* (Chicago,III,. 1964), p.17..
6. Tucci,n.2,p.231.

place and was subject to extension. It was, however, without a doctrinal structure.

Recent researches indicate that the term *"Bon"* consists of two members. The first means to invoke, being related to *"Bod pa"* which means to invoke or to invite; the second means seed. There is also the Shang shung term *"gyer"* which means to chant. According to this difinition, a *Bon po* is an invoker (of the gods) and hence one who chants. The second difinition is perhaps related to the variant form of the word found in the Tung huang manuscripts, i.e. to the more usual *"Bod"*. *"Bon"* may, therefore, be taken to mean the autochthonous Tibetan religion. On this basis a *Bon po* in pre-Buddhist times was the one who invoked, i.e. a particular type of priest among several others. There were different kinds of *Bon po*. There were *Bon po* of gods, of men, of horses, of magic, of heaven, of the created world, of the paternal clan, of burials, etc, according to their specialization. Each clan had its own *Bon po*. Priests known as *gShen* were Shamans according to Professor Hoffman, but they were sacrificers according to Snellgrove. They too are classified variously like the *Bon po*.[7]

According to Professor Namkhai Norbu, *"Bon"* is an ancient Tibetan term and is identical in meaning with *"bzla"*, which is to recite *mantras* or magic formulae (*sNgag*).[8] In ancient records the word is sometimes replaced by the word *"gyer"*. The term *"Bon"* owes its origin to the recitation of mantras by the ancient *Bon po* to ward off the cause of obstacles (illnesses etc.) and to

7. Per Kvaerne, "The Genesis of the Tibetan Buddhist Tradition", *Tibetan Review* (New Delhi), March 1976, p.11.
8. Namkhai Norbu, "Bon and Bonpos", ibid., December 1980, p.8.

obtain the capacity for fierce action. Professor Namkhai Norbu cites in support of his definition the invasion of Tibet by the Dzungars in A.D.1727 when many *rNying ma pa* and *Bon po* were executed. Later, when the Tibetans went to meet Dzungar officials, they were made to stick out their tongues to show that they were indeed not *rNying ma pa* or *Bon po*. The tongues of most of them had turned black or brown because of their repeated recitations of mantras. The Tibetans kept up this habit of sticking out their tongues as a mark of respect whenever they met a high lama or a Government official. Professor Namkhai Norbu mentions priests of another type, viz. the *sShen*, the name by which the stock of gShen rab mi bo, the traditional founder of the *Bon* religion, is known. He is of the opinion that Western Tibetologists are wrong in holding that Shamanism is a corruption of the word "*gShen*" and that it originated from *Bon*. The *gShen* were already well known in Tibet when Lord gShen rab mi bo was born.

Priests of the *Bon* religion were very much a part of the pre- Buddhist Tibet. A unified system making up the *Bon* religion came at a much later stage, perhaps in the wake of the advent of a foreign religion, viz. Buddhism, about the seventh century. A believer in *Bon* is called a *Bon po*. To a believer the word "Bon" signifies truth, the reality, or the eternal, unchanging doctrine centring on truth and reality. The word "Bon" has the same connotation for the adherents of that religion as the word "*Chos*" (corresponding to the Sanskrit word "*Dharma*") has for the Buddhists. In fact there is no word for Buddhism in Tibet. The Tibetans are known either as *Chos pa* (followers of *Chos* or Dharma) or as *Bon po* (followers of Bon). The term "*Sangs rgyas*" (literally "amply purified") signifies the Buddha of the *Bon po*.

The early history of the *Bon* religion and the character of that religion are still not clear owing to lack of authentic documentary evidence. We have no documents dating back to those early days; for it was only in the first half of the seventh century that Tibet was blessed with a literary language and developed a literature. What we do have are Buddhist and *Bon po* works belonging to the twelfth century or after. These give only a sketchy account, together with general ideas about the *Bon* beliefs. Moreover, they are not entirely unbiassed. The Tung huang manuscripts go back to the ninth and tenth centurires or even a little earlier, but give only a fragmentary, not a systematic, account of *Bon*. There are some later chronicles which record tradition as faithfully transmitted down the centuries. Finally there is some information to be had in the Chinese chronicles of the Tang dynasty. Let us see what facts we can put together from these sources.[9]

Division of the World and Its Divinities

According to ancient Tibetan belief, the world is divided into three spheres - heaven, air, and earth or heaven, earth, and the underworld. The underworld is peopled by spirits of various kinds - as for instance, the *klu* which can assume the form of snakes at will. The *klu* live in rivers and lakes and even wells and guard the treasures hidden there. Then there are the *gNyan* which live in trees or among rocks. They are easily annoyed and send sickness and death by way of retaliation. Plague

9. Helmut Hoffman, *The Religions of Tibet,* Edward Firzgerald, trans.(London, 1961), edn 2, pp.16-17.

is a scourge attributed to the *gNyan* in particular. As they prefer to roam on mountains, they are allied to mountain gods. On the earth proper there are the *Sa bdag,* or masters of the earth, and vampires known as *Sri,* which prey on small childern. The air is the domain of the *bTsan* which appear as savage huntsmen, red in colour, wearing helmets and armour, and riding light red horses over mountains under the leadership of their king. If a man happens to cross their path in the loneliness of mountains, they pierce him with their arrows or he is overtaken by a deadly disease.

Heaven

The *Bon po* hold heaven in high honour. The king of heaven is surrounded by a host of supernatural beings- by gods and other spirits (*dmu*, *Then rang*, and *bDud*). Heaven consists of nine strata, later raised to thirteen. To go from one stratum to the next a sky ladder is necessary. As we have seen already, the first king of Tibet came from heaven to his people by means of such a sky ladder. After having fulfilled their earthly tasks, the first seven kings returned to heaven by the same means. The eighth of this line was Gri gum who inadvertently cut the sky ladder while engaged in a contest with his minister. He was, therefore, unable to return to heaven. At his death he left his body on earth. Since then the Tibetans have observed burial rites.

Gods of Everyday life

In addition there are gods connected with man's everyday life- like the ones that preside over his fields, tents, hearths and homes, etc.

The god presiding over mans's hearth and home is the one needing special propitiation as he is easily annoyed. One way of pleasing him is to offer him butter. It is a great offence if a hair, or an old rag, or a dog's dirt finds its way into the fire or if a pot boils over and dirties the hearth. To ward off the dangers of the god's displeasure the owner of the house calls in an experienced priest to perform the appropriate cleaning rites. The hearth is dug out, and the priest goes into a trance to find out the cause of pollution. He takes a lump of earth and examines it. If a living insect is found in it, it is destroyed immediately. If no living thing is found in the lump of earth, the owner is in a perilous state; for it means that the demon causing pollution has made good his escape and the priest is in no position to help.

Guardian Angels

Two spirits, *pho lha* and *dgra lha*, serve as guardian angels to ward off evil influences. It is believed that the spirit *pho lha* is an ancestor watching over the family fortunes and that *dgra lha* deals with the enemies of the family. If these two spirits leave the body of a man for some reason, he turns susceptible to attack by evil spirits and falls a prey to disease. An experienced priest is then called in to conjure the guardian spirits back. If the guardian spirits do not come back, the man is sure to die. It is believed that Gri gum, the eighth king of the first dynasty, was easily killed by his enemy because both his guardian spirits were then absent. They had left his body for some reason, leaving him unprotected.

Spirit Traps

Certain spirits are regarded as appearing in the form of winged insects. To ward off the attention of such winged insects, the Tibetans have devised spirit traps known as *mDos*. These traps catch all evil spirits as does a spider's web. They consist of two or more sticks on which threads of different colours are woven. These come in every shape and size. When the priest confirms that the spirits have been caught, the spirit traps are burnt down.

Animal Sacrifices

Sacrifice of animals to propitiate gods was an important feature of the old *Bon* religion. Such sacrifice was performed in State ceremonies like the taking of oath of fealty or at the time of the signing of treaties. Sheep, dogs, donkeys, horses, yaks, and sometimes even human beings were sacrificed to please the gods of heaven and earth. Vivid descriptions of instances of human sacrifice are available in *Bon* texts like *gZer myig*. To bring about the recovery of a prince who had fallen ill one of his subjects was sacrificed. At the time of the 3-yearly oath-taking ceremonies performed to affirm their loyalty to the king the chiefs of various clans sacrificed human beings along with a large number of other animals.

Death Rites

The old *Bon* religion had elaborate death rites. These rites started with the death of King Gri gum who, as we have already seen, left his body behind on the earth when he died, having cut the sky ladder inadvertently and thereby deprived himself of the means of ascending to heaven along with his body at the end of his life. As the Tibetan priests of those days were not sufficiently acquainted with the appropriate burial rites, three *Bon* priests were sent for from *Kha che*, *Bru sha*, and *Shang shung*. One of these priests was an expert in burial rites and carried out an operation known as *Taming of the Dead,* apparently with a magic knife. The aim of these rites was probably to prevent the spirits of the dead from returning to the earth and harming the living. Subsquently the *Bon po* codified these rites and laid down three hundred and sixty ways of dying, four ways of preparing graves, and eightyone ways of taming evil spirits.

Concern with the Continuance of Life after Death

The *Bon* religion seems to have been preoccupied with the idea of life after death; for it had elaborate rituals meant to ensure that the soul of a dead man was conducted safely to the land of bliss by an appropriate animal, usually a yak, a horse, or a sheep which was sacrificed in the course of the funerary rites. Offerings of food, drink, and precious objects were likewise made to accompany the dead. The rites were most elaborate in the case of the death of a king or a high nobleman when his close associates were also buried with him. This rite was subsequently changed so as to make the close associates of the king live in the precincts of the tomb as its keepers and protectors. They were in fact consecrated as the subjects of the corpse of the king. A distinction was made between the living and the dead in that they lived apart from other men. They did not come into contact with any living member of the royal line, and, except at the time of worship, no living man, horse, or cattle was allowed to wander in the outer enclosure of the grave. If some men or animals strayed into the forbidden area around the grave, they were seized by the keepers of the grave. If they were touched by the keepers of the grave, they could not thereafter return to the company of the living. They were also marked as dead, and they became servants of the keepers of the grave. The keepers of the grave had no work to do for others. They protected the treasure in the chamber in which the dead body lay. An enormous mound was raised over the grave. A large number of priests and court officials were involved in the burial rites. The rites took several years to be completed. They were meant to ensure the happiness of the deceased in the land of the dead and to secure their beneficial influence for the welfare and fertility of the living.

Shrines and Architecture

Although the *Bon* religion had a highly complicated ritualistic system, its religious architecture appears to have been very modest. It does not seem to have had any temples and monasteries. There are of course references to some spiritual centres or shrines in the books. A large number of priests and sorcerers were employed to service the community. There are references to their specialized functions in different fields, including occult and oracular matters. The *gShen* were the most important among the priests. The word "*gShen*" is associated with the name of the mythical founder of the *Bon* religion, viz. gShen rab mi bo. In fact the word "*gShen rab*" means only "the pre-eminent gShen". It is no proper name at all.

It would thus appear that the Tibetans in the ancient days believed their kings to be of divine origin probably in view of their descent from the sky. Belief in the divine nature of their kings and their gods, especially the gods of mountains, originally formed the nucleus of their religious system. There were then priests who performed various rituals and conducted solemn ceremonies on special occasions such as the enthronement of a king and the

10. David L.Snellgrove and Hugh E.Richardson, *A Cultural History of Tibet* (Boulder, Colo.,1980), p.52.
11. Hoffman,n.9, p.25.

signing of a treaty. These priests were known as *gShen* or *Bon po*, and the rituals they performed went by the name of *Bon*. Belief in the divine nature of the Tibetan kings and the rituals performed by way of worship of the gods were in fact the essential part of *Bon*. The existence of a large number of funerary rituals, a hierarchy of priests, and a belief in the divine nature of kings and in some kind of life after death clearly suggest that the *Bon* religion was more complex than we are generally inclined to grant. In the seventh century *Bon* was already adopting foreign elements. The influence of Iran on its cosmogony is well known. Towards the end of the seventh century A.D., Tibet was one of the strongest Powers in Central Asia, striving with Buddhist rulers for pre-eminence. As certain territories came under Tibetan rule, the Tibetans who were put in charge of those territories came into direct contact with Buddhism. *Bon*, therefore, was exposed directly to Buddhist influence.[12]

Evolution of Bon

The development of *Bon* from a tribal cult in ancient Tibet into its present highly evolved form with its own body of literature, doctrines, monasteries, monks, teachings, and rules of discipline took place in stages. According to a learned Buddhist scholar, rJe btsun blo bzang chos kyi nyi ma dpal bzang po of the eighteeth century A.D., there were three stages.[13]

---

12. Samten G.Karmay, *A General Introduction to the History and Doctrines of Bon* (Tokyo, 1975), p.182.
13. Sarat Chandra Dass, *Contribution on the Religious History of Tibet* (New Delhi, 1970), p.10.

Jola Bon (rDol bon) or Revealed Bon

During the reign of King Khri lde brtsan po, the sixth in descent from King gNya, khri brtsan po, a goblin kidnapped a boy of thirteen belonging to a *gShen* family and took him to different places and mountains of Tibet and Kham. The boy wandered thus for thirteen years and was fully instructed in the demonic arts. At the age of twentysix he was eventually allowed to return to his native place. Thanks to his training and his travels, he knew the haunts of malicious spirits, goblins, and demons. He could tell which of the spirits committed mischief and which of them brought good luck, as also the ways of appeasing hostile spirits by means of rituals and offerings. Thus this young man first introduced *Bon* into Tibet. All Tibetan kings from gNya' khri brtsan po down wards followed *Bon* and no other religion.

The *Bon po* of that age were skilled in witchcraft, in the performance of mystical rites for suppressing evil spirits and cannibalistic hobgoblins of the nether regions, in the propitiation of the venerable gods above, and in the conduct of domestic ceremonies aimed at appeasing the malignant spirits of the middle region (earth) and ensuring that they did not pollute the hearth. There were no other theories concerning the *Bon* religion at the time. This stage is called *Gyu bon chab nag*, i.e. the original *Bon* of the Dark Valley or the Dark Ages.

Stein relates a variant of this story which is attributed to a sixteenth-century historian.[14] At On in Central Tibet (Amsho district) a boy of twelve (or thirteen) belonging to the *gShen* clan was found to have the ears of a donkey. A demon carried him off and took him all over Tibet for twelve or thirteen years. When the boy, now a young

14. Stein, n.3, p.233.

man, eventually came back, he knew not only the names of numerous demons but also the places they lived in. To hide his donkey's ears he wore a woollen turban. Such a turban is now a distinctive mark of *Bon*, and the legend is used to explain why it is worn. The *Bon po* who claim descent from this donkey-eared ancestor are said to be experts in a number of rituals: "Below they tamed the demon, above they worshipped the god of the ancients [or of the old, *rgan lha*-probably ancestors], and in the middle they purified the hearth in the event of pollution."

At this stage of development the rituals were aimed at obtaining protection and assistance on behalf of the king, the tribal chieftains, and the privileged families against the forces of evil in situations of crisis. Later they provided the basis for raising a doctrinal superstructure.

Khyar Bon or Deviant Bon

This second stage in the development or evolution of *Bon* is marked by innovations introduced on account of foreign influence. As we have seen, when King Gri gum was killed, the old Tibetan priests did not know what funerary rites to perform in order to prevent the spirit of the dead from doing mischief to the living. They, therefore, invited three *Bon* priests-one from *Kha che*, the second from *Bru sha*, and the third from *Shang shung*-to perform the burial rites. Traditions vary on the names of the original countries of these *Bon* priests. According to one source, one of them was a native of the land of *Gurnawatra* situated between India and Iran. According to another source, he came from *Ashas* (i.e. the country of the Turco-Mongols of Koko Nor) whose specialization lay in worshipping the gods on behalf of

15. Tucci, n.2, p.214.

the living and subdue the demons for the good of the dead. What is important to note is that all three were foreigners and came from countries which lay west of Tibet. The origin of an important branch of *Bon* would thus be sited in the southwest, in countries where the influence of India and Iran converged. One of the priests was able to travel in the sky mounted on a tambourine and discover mines. He could also perform other miracles:he could cut iron or stone with a feather. He offered meat and alcohol to the demons to propitiate them. The king made him his *bla mchod* (chaplain) and conferred high authority on him. His insignia of office consisted of a turquoise *swastika*, a tiger skin, and a sword. The second was skilled in divination. He could decipher mystic symbols and tell the future. For this purpose he employed strings (*ju thig*), a scapula (*sog dmar*), and his own inspired, oracular utterances (*lha bka'*). The third was an expert in funerary rites, particularly for those killed by the sword. It was probably a matter of exorcising or appeasing "certain souls" for the sake of the dead man.[16]

rJe btsan cho kyi nyi ma considers that this was the beginning of *Bon* as a philosophical system and that its new status was due to the influence of the heretical *Śaivite* doctrine. Other foreign *Bon po* too played a part. King Drong nyen deru, the great- grandfather of Srong brtsan sgam po, sent for a physician from the country of *Ashas* who was a *Bon po* from *Sumpa* country to cure him of an illness. The mother of this priest was Chinese. Even King Srong brtsan sgam po, who was a patron of Buddhism, did not neglect *Bon*. He is stated to have

16. Stein, n.3, p.231.

brought *Lha dem*, a *Bon po*, from Shang shung and put him in the school of *Awa namse*, also a Bon po. They devoted themselves to divining the causes of illnesses, invoking the gods, and exorcising demons. As the priests taught one another in this way, *Bon* too was diffused. It adapted itself to forms which were more Tibetan than foreign.

This phase in the evolution of *Bon* marks the beginning of a period of development in theory and organization and of contact with other religious centres, including those which lay outside Tibet. The *Śaivite* influence mentioned by rJe btsan cho kyi nyi ma probably came from a *Śaivite yogī* or siddha.

bsGyur Bon or Modified Bon

This stage may be said to consist of three substages: (i) An Indian scholar, expelled for some profane or immoral act, went to the north of Kashmir dressed in a blue robe and there wrote some heretical works and hid them under the ground. After a few years, he invited the public to witness the discovery by him of some ancient religious works and dug out the works which he had hidden. By proclaiming them as *Bon* literature, he brought about a change in the *Bon* religion. (ii) During the reign of King Khri srong lde brtsan an edict was issued requiring all *Bon po* to renounce their faith and embrace Buddhism. A *Bon* priest named Rin chen mchog did not consent to fall in line and was punished. Thereupon the priest, along with other *Bon po*, composed *Bon* scriptures with the help of Buddhist canonical works. When the King learnt that the excellent sayings of the Buddha had been incorporated into *Bon* scriptures, he felt outraged and had the priests concerned beheaded. He had many other *Bon po* too killed. Those who survived the purge made many copies of their works and concealed them under rocks. Later they reclaimed them. These are called *Bon gter ma* ("hidden treasure of the *Bon po*"). (iii) Subsequent to the overthrow of Buddhism by gLang dar ma in the ninth century, some *Bon* priests altered many Buddhist works by using an orthography and a terminology different from those of the Buddhists. Two of them, Sen gyur and Dar yul dolag from Upper *gNyan* in Tsang, composed their works, sitting in a solitary cavern in U (dBus) consecrated as the Centre of *Bon* religion. Later they hid their works under rocks. After some time they brought them out of the various hiding places as if they were accidental discoveries. Other priests also converted many Buddhist works into *Bon* scriptures.

These three substages of the third stage, known as *bsGyurpa* bon, are designated *Chab kar*, or *Dapui bon*, meaning "the white water [the enlightened *Bon*] or the resultant *Bon*". This our account is based on the writings of a learned Buddhist lama of the eighteenth century. A bias cannot, therefore, be ruled out.

Conflict with Buddhism

By the beginning of the eighth century *Bon* was powerful enough to oppose the official introduction of Buddhism into Tibet. King Khri srong lde brtsan was an ardent Buddhist, but his chief wife was a *Bon po*. She was the only one of his several wives to bear him sons. Her love of the *Bon* religion was so great that she poisoned one of her own sons when she found that he was becoming too enthusiastic about Buddhism. The *Bon po* tradition maintains that she had her husband also killed by means of magic. On her side there were many influential ministers, one of them being Ngan stag ra klu gong. His services to his king and country were so highly esteemed that a specially inscribed stone pillar was erected in his honour in the year 760 A.D., This pillar still stands in front of the *Potala* in Lhasa.[17]

The *Bon* religion developed in West Tibet, particularly in Shang shung, under the influence of not only Buddhism but also Zoroastrian and Manichaen teachings, into a syncretist system with a well-developed doctrine and literature. It was this systematized Bon religion that the Tibetan nobles encouraged in their political struggle against the dynasty and against Buddhism. They brought in priests from Shang shung and made them translate their texts into Tibetan. They did their utmost to make the *Bon* religion the State religion of Tibet. Their greed for political power was often disguised by religious disputation. One faction even managed to get a ban placed on Buddhism temporarily when King Khri srong lde brtsan was still a minor.

All sources are agreed that Shang shung played an important part in the development and syncretization of the *Bon* religion. Tradition assigns an enormous area to this country extending up to *Bru sha* in the west, Li in the north, Dangs ra Khyung rdzong in the east, and Chu mig brgyad cu rtsa gnyis in the south; sTag gzigs formed the inner region. It is not certain that it embraced such a vast area, but it did cover the whole of West Tibet and was an independent kingdom. Its capital was Khyung lung dngul mkhar, which lay to the west of Mount *Ti se*. In the seventh century AD it appears to have had a king called Lig myi rhya. One of his wives was a sister of the Tibetan king. Then King Srong brtsan sgam po annexed the country to Tibet. (Or was it King Khri srong lde brtsan in the eighth century? Accounts vary.) After being

17. Karmay, n. 12, pp.181-3.

annexed to Tibet, Shang shung was gradually Tibetanized. And it contributed much to the development of Tibetan culture, being Tibet's nearest neighbour; it was also open to influence from sTag gzigs, Bru sha, Li, and other Central Asian countries. Its own culture and language were integrated into those of Tibet. Perhaps its religion too underwent a similar change. The people worshipped *sKu bla ge khod*, who, they believed, lived on *Mount Ti se*. According to *Bon po* tradition, it was through Shang shung that the teaching of gShen rab mi bo was brought to Tibet. The teaching was originally in the language of Shang shung, but was later translated into Tibetan. Let us now go into the origin of *Bon*, the teacher gShen rab mi bo, his teaching, and the origianl beliefs, practices, and observances according to *Bon po* tradition.[18]

Place of Origin

Bon po tradition maintains that the ultimate source of *Bon* is the land of *'Ol mo lung ring*. This is said to be a part of sTag gzigs, identified by scholars as Iran. It is imperishable. When this world is ultimately consumed by fire, it will raise itself up to the sky and unite with another holy land in the heavens called *Srid pa ye sangs*. The idea of an indestructible and yet material world is not peculiar to *Bon*. In Buddhism also *Vajrasana* rises to the sky when this world perishes.

It is believed that *'Ol mo lung ring,* which is situated vaguely somewhere in the west, occupies one-third of this world. It takes the form of an eight-petalled flower, with the sky too corresesopondingly taking the shape of a wheel with eight spokes. The land is dominated by Mount gYung drung dgu brtsegs. This name means, literally, "pile of

18. Ibid., pp.172-9.

nine *swastikas* representing the *Nine Ways of Bon*". Both the *swastika* and the number nine are of great significance. The swastika, which corresponds to the *vajra* in Buddhism, is the symbol of indestructibility. In ancient inscriptions the word *"gYung drung du"*, which means *swastika*, is often used as an adverb, with the particle *"du"*. *gYung drung du* means "always" or "permanently". The compound is an epithet of *Bon; 'phrul ngag gYung drung Bon* means "the magic word everlasting *Bon*". The number nine is connected with the earth, the heavens, and the *Bon* doctrine. The earth has nine layers from the crust downwards (*sa rim pa dgu*). The heavens originally had nine stages (*gnam rim pa dgu*), but later expanded, so that they now have thirteen-another auspicious number in *Bon*. The *Bon* doctrine is also classified under nine different heads (*theg pa rim pa dgu*). The nine stages of Mount gYung drung dgu brtsegs represent the Nine Ways of Bon. The peak of the mountain is in the form of a crystal monolith. Four rivers flow from its base in four directions: in the east the river *Nara* issues from a rock shaped like the mouth of a lion; in the north the river *Pakshu* flows out of a rock which looks like the mouth of a horse; in the west the river *Kyim shang* arises from what appears to be the mouth of a peacock; and in the south the river *Sin dhu* springs from what one might mistake for the mouth of an elephant. There are hundreds of temples, cities, and parks in the vicinity of the mountain, but only eight are noteworthy.

The land consists of three regions. In the inner region are located the important temple of Sham po lha rtse, the palace where gShen rab mi bo was born, and another two palaces. In these two palaces there lived gShen rab mi bo's two wives and six childern (three childern by each wife). In addition to the four centres (i.e.the temple and the three palaces) Mount gYung drung dgu brtsegs also forms part of the inner region. The intermediate region contains twelve cities. Then there is the outer region. The three regions are divided by rivers and lakes, and the whole land is skirted by an ocean called *Mu Khyud bdal ba'i rgya mtsho* "Spreading Ocean of Enclosure". It was in this ocean to the west of 'Ol mo lung ring that Kong tse 'Phrul gyi rgyal po built his miraculous temple. According to tradition, he was a Chinese king and a follower of gShen rab mi bo. The temple became a very important place: it was there that the chief disciples of gShen rab mi bo gathered together all his teachings, wrote them down, and deposited them.

The ocean *Mu Khyud bdal ba'i rgya mtsho* is enclosed in a circle of snow-covered mountains called *dBal so gangs kyi ra ba*, or the wall of sharp snow-covered mountains. This is similar to the name that the Tibetans sometimes used for their country, viz *Gangs ri'i ra bskor bai zing khams* ("Land Ringed Round by a Wall of Snow-covered Mountains).

Access to 'Ol mo lung ring is via the route created by gShen rab when he paid a visit to Tibet by shooting an arrow through the mountain and carving out a big tunnel along the path taken by the arrow. To pass through this tunnel, however, is not an easy matter. There are many gorges and wild beasts on the way. Moreover, the tunnel is quite dark. Generally it takes nine days to traverse the entire length of it.

What is given here is not even a fraction of the elaborate description one finds in the various *Bon po* works. So far we have not found any evidence in the manuscripts or inscriptions available in support of any name or even idea of a land called 'Ol mo lung ring within the limits of sTag gzigs or within Shang shung before the tenth century. In fact no archaeological excavation or systematic collection of manuscripts has yet been carried out in Tibet. The period from the collapse of the Tibetan kingdom following the assassination of King gLang dar ma to the beginning of the tenth century A.D., can be called the darkest period in Tibetan history. The country was in political and religious confusion. It was in the beginning of the tenth century A.D, that Buddhism was revived in Tibet. Buddhist texts brought from India were translated. This apparently inspired the *Bon po* to review their own position. They felt that their religion could not have originated in an ordinary place. They, therefore, started regarding sTag gzigs as the country which contained 'Ol mo lung ring, the birthplace of gShen rab. They were all admiration for the culture and civilization of sTag gzigs.

However, if one considers carefully the descriptions given in the scriptures of the mountains and rivers in 'Ol mo lung ring in the light of modern geographical knowledge, one gets the feeling that Mount *Ti se,* with rivers flowing away from its base, may very well be identical with *Mount gYung drung dgu brtsegs*. This is so because Mount *Ti se* was the most important centre of Shang shung which is, according to tradition, the place of origin of *Bon*. Second, there are important *Bon po* texts written in both the language of Shang shung and Tibetan. Although some scholars are inclined to believe that Shang shung was an artificial language created by the *Bon po* to accord with *Sanskrit*, the second language of Buddhism in Tibet, the presence of large numbers of Shang shung words in modern Ladakhi and Kunawari in the old western region of Tibet points to the reality of the Shang shung language.

And yet we shall do well to refrain from identifying '*Ol mo lung ring* with Mount *Ti se* and its vicinity; for the believers consider this region to be too ordinary to be the birthplace of gShen rab although they grant that it is the holy land of *Bon*. Perhaps they prefer that the birthplace of gShen rab is an unknown, mystic land which exists only on the spiritual plane. In 1964, on the basis of the descriptions given of the land in the scriptures, Tenzin Namdak, a *Bon po* scholar, prepared a small booklet on *Bon po* chronology, together with a vocabulary of the Shang shung language with Tibetan equivalents. He also included in his booklet a map illustrating the traditional representation of 'Ol mo lung ring. According to some scholars, this map is close to that of sTag gzigs and the Middle East, thus bearing out Bon po tradition.

gShen rab mi bo

gShen rab is the founder of the *Bon* religion and occupies a position very similar to that of the Buddha. There is, however, no material on the basis of which we may establish his historicity or his racial origin, or the authenticity of the vast literature attributed to him. According to *Bon po* tradition, his teaching was written down after his death in the same way that the Buddhist scriptures were compiled. After the tenth century A.D., however, facts and legends were woven together to form an idea of his life.

There are three versions of the life of gShen rab. First, there is what is called *mDo dus*. This is the earliest known version of the life of gShen rab. It is also the shortest of all versions and contains twentyone chapters. It is considered to be a translation from the language of Shang shung. It is classified as *gter ma*, i.e. a rediscovered text. Its discovery goes back to the tenth century A.D.

Another account is *gZer myig*, which is in two volumes of eighteen chapters. It is also classified as *gter ma*. It is considered to be the most important work among the *Bon po* scriptures. Its date is generally given as the eleventh century A.D.,

A third version of gShen rab's life is known as *gZi brjid*, which is in twelve volumes. Hence it is the longest of the three. It belongs to the category of *snyan brgyud* or oral transmission. That is to say, it is a text dictated by a sage or divinity to an amanuensis. Some people believe that it was dictated to Blo ldan snying po in the fourteenth century A.D., If so, it would be the latest version. It is considered to be an extended version of *gZer myig* and contains extensive material of ancient origin on a wide range of subjects such as customs, stories about birds and beasts, and the like that is not found in *gZer myig*. It is an epic rather than a hagiographical work.

Now for an outline of the life of gShen rab. In the heaven Srid pa ye sangs there were three brothers Dag pa, gSal ba, and Shes pa. They studied *Bon* under Bum khri glong gi lce can, a *Bon po* sage. Then they all went to the god gShen lha 'od dkar to ask him what they should do to relieve the misery of mankind. The god told them that they should each work in three successive ages as the Guide. Accordingly the first brother, Dag pa, served as the Guide in the Age Past. The second brother, gSal ba, came down as gShen rab to serve as the Guide in the Age Present. The third brother, Shes pa, will come down to take up the work of guiding in the age that is yet to come. The god promised gShen rab that he would be his supervisor. Another god, Srid pa sangs po 'bum khri, agreed to assist him in the maintenance of world order. (These three constitute the *Bon po triad* and are knwon as Lha, gShen, and Srid pa.)

gShen rab took birth in 'Ol mo lung ring as a prince. He started preaching while still a child. Throughout his life the demon Khyab pa lag ring was his rival, a relationship similar to the one between the Buddha and Devadatta. One of the most important events of gShen rab's life was the visit he is said to have paid to Tibet, not because he wanted to preach *Bon*, but because his seven horses were stolen by Khyab pa lag ring. However, once in Tibet, he took the opportunity to preach *Bon* there. He found that the Tibetans were not yet ready to receive his teaching in full. He prophesied that his teaching would spread from 'Ol mo lung ring to all of Tibet in future. The demon Khyab pa lag ring tried to deter gShen rab by taking terrifying forms, but the more he tried to strike terror the less effective he turned out to be. Finally he surrendered and became one of the followers of gShen rab. Eventually gShen rab withdrew to a cave for quiet contemplation. He died at the age of eightytwo.

The whole life of gShen rab as given in these texts is conceived within the framework of twelve acts. It can be compared to the life of the Buddha who too is said to have performed twelve acts. It is thus apparent that in these versions of gShen rab's life the influence of Buddhism is constantly present. Buddhist thought is interwoven in the narrative. The idea of cause and effect (*karma*), rebirth, the essentialy miserable nature of life, the method of escape from it, and the idea of enlightenment are all there. gShen rab is represented as a superhuman being whose only purpose in taking birth in this world was to preach *Bon* and guide all living beings to a better world.

Accounts dating back to a period earlier than the tenth century A.D., are contained in the Tung huang manuscripts of the ninth century A.D., or even earlier.

gShen rab is mentioned five times as a sort of priest. Though not an important figure, he is represented there as an indispensable priest who had the capacity of communicating with the dead as well as the living. It may be inferred from these accounts that such a person did exist and that he was of Tibetan origin. Probably he lived before the seventh century A. D.. *Bon po* chronology represents him as having lived even earlier than the Buddha. The glorification of gShen rab may be compared to the deification of the historical Buddha in the Mahāyāna tradition.

Teaching of gShen rab

gShen rab mi bo is believed to have taught two main systems. First, there is the system of *sGo bzhi mdzod* lnga, i.e. the Four Portals (or Ways) and One Treasury. The Four Portals are (1) *Chab dkar,* or white water, signifying the esoteric teaching (mainly spells); (2) *Chab nag*, or black water, consisting of narratives and rituals; (3)' *Phan yul* embraces all the exoteric teaching-as, for example, monastic discipline; and (4) *dPon gsas*, or direct and special precepts to aid in doing psycho-spiritual exercises such as the system of *rDzogs chen* meditation. The Treasury, also known as the Summit, is called *mThog thog* or *sPyi rgyugs.* It literally means that it runs into all the Four Portals.

One may see here that there is direct correspondence with Buddhist classification. The first corresponds to the *tantras,* and the third to the *sūtras.*

Another system of classification is *Theg pa dgu,* which is translated as Nine Ways or Vehicles. These are further divided into three categories. The first four ways are the Ways of Cause (*rgyu'u theg pa*); and second four are the Ways of Result (*'bras b'ui theg pa*); and the ninth is the system of *rDzogs chen* meditation. Briefly the contents of the Nine Ways[19] are as follows: (1) The Way of the gShen of Prediction (*Phyva gshen theg pa*). This describes four different ways of prediction: (a) sortilege (*mo*); (b) astrological calculation (*rtsis*); (c) ritual (*gto*); and (d) medical diagnosis or examination of causes (*dpyad*). (2) The Way of the gShen of the Visual World (*sNang gshen theg pa*). This explains the origin and nature of the gods and demons living in this world, the methods of performing exorcism, and ransom of various kinds. (3) The Way of the gShen of Illusion (*'phrul gshen theg pa*). This is concerned with rites of disposing of enemies of all kinds. These rites are to be found in the *Bon tantras*. Similar practices are to be found in the Buddhist *tantras* too. (4) The Way of the gShen of Existence (*Srid gshen theg pa*). This deals with beings in the intermediate stage (*bar do*), i.e. between death and rebirth, and with the ways of working out one's salvation or achieving a better rebirth. (5) The Way of the Virtuous Adherents (*dGe bsnen theg pa*). This guides those who follow the ten virtues and the ten perfections. *dGe bsnen* is the normal Tibetan term for the Buddhist layman. (6) The Way of the Great Ascetics (*Drang srong theg pa*). This is used by the *Bon po* to refer to fully qualified monks corresponding to Buddhist *bhikkus*. The reference is to their strict ascetic discipline. (7) The Way of Pure Sound (*Adkar theg pa*). This deals with the higher *tantric* practices. It has to do with the *tantric* theory of transformation through what is called the *mandala* and with the union of method and wisdom as realized by the *tantric* and his feminine partner. There are nine "reliances", eighteen "performances", and nine "acts". A "reliance" comprises a primary need, a "performance"

19. Snellgrove, n.4,pp.9-11; and Tadeusz sKorupsky, "Tibetan gYung drung Monastery at Dolanji", *Kailash* (Kathmandu), vol.8, nos 1-2, 1981, pp.29-35.

refers to the whole process of *mandala,* and an "act" represents the total power that accrues to one from mastering all the Nine Vehicles. (8) The Way of the Primaeval gShen (Ye gShen theg pa). This deals with the selection of a suitable master, a suitable partner, and a suitable site and the preparation of the *mandala,* together with important admonitions, such as the admonition not to forget local divinities (*sa bdags*). It recounts the process of meditation (known as the process of examination) and describes the normal way of worshipping the great beings in any Tibetan temple, *Bon* or Buddhist. It also touches upon the process of realization, which is the "super-rational" state of a perfected sage. The behaviour of such a sage is often mistaken for that of a mad man. (9) The Supreme Way (*bLa med theg pa*). This describes the absolute, referred to as the basis (*gzi,* corresponding to the Sanskrit word "*alaya*"). There are two concepts here, the concept of release and the concept of delusion. Release is the state of the fivefold Buddhahood; delusion is the false understanding of erring beings in the intermediate state (*bar do*). The way is described as mind in its absolute state, or as pure thought or enlightenment. The fruit or final effect is to be described in terms of the special powers of a perfected sage. The whole subject matter is covered by the four conventional headings of insight, contemplation, practice, and achievement. The categories and ideas elaborated are usually referred to as the teaching of the Great Perfection (*rDzogs chen*).

The *Bon* scriptures[20] state that the normal length of life of a human being was immeasurable at the start of the present *kalpa*; it will be just ten years when the *kalpa* ends. There will be altogether eighteen divine manifestations in this *kalpa*, from Kun tu bzang po, the

20. Dass, n.13, pp.9-10 and 15-19.

chief *Bon* god, to Than ma medon. Of these manifestations, gShen rab, who is said to have appeared when the normal length of life of a human being had declined to a hundred years, is regarded as the reigning *Bon* god. The *Bon po* believe that he was born in 'Ol mo lung ring in the country of Shang shung. Some authors opine that, being a miraculous incarnation of the Buddha, he was contemporaneous with the latter.

The Buddha became incarnate as gShen rab in Shang shung to bring about moral improvement of the *Bon po.* He observed the twelve acts of *Bon* and taught the Nine Ways or Vehicles of Knowledge, opened the door of the abode of the gods of the living, shut the entrance of the graves of the dead, and committed the living to the path of *swastika* (*gYung drung*). He possessed foreknowledge and performed miracles. He visited many places of *Bon* pilgrimage in Tibet. He subdued demons and evil spirits. He bound them all under solemn oath. He explained the four ways of the *swastika* and *skanda* and the five repositories of the sacred scriptures. Six of his spiritual descendants bore the surname of *Mu tsho* and *lDem.* They were: the sage Mu tsho tra he si of sTag gzigs; the sage Devanātha, surnamed Mantra Ushma, of India; the sage Legs tang mang of China; the sage of Khrom gser rdog lce 'byams, the sage lDem gyen tsha smang of Tibet; the sage lCe tsha gargu of Myanmar; the learned Mu 'spang gsang tang of the Sum pa country; and the sage Sher bu chen of Shang shung. These and many other followers conveyed the *Bon* teachings to all quarters.

The countries associated in the work of syncretization or systematization of the *Bon* religion were thus China, India, Myanmar, Shang shung, Sum pa, and sTag gzigs, besides Tibet.

The *Bon* scriptures teach love and compassion and the unsteadiness (impermanence) of all things. They also teach *karma* and *phala*. They exalt the Bodhisattva feeling, the five ways of emancipation, the ten stages of perfection, and the names of the three images. Besides, they speak of inauguration, formation, and perfection (ceremonies), vows, sanctification (consecration), and sacrifice, the construction of circles and the figure of mystic worship, and funerary and other rites. Many of the rites are similar to the ones practiced by the Buddhists in form and nature. However, the *Bon po* occasionally differ with the Buddhists in their orthography, rhetoric, and syntax. In doctrinal and meditative matters the *Bon po* are divided into the heretical and the orthodox.

A *Bon* work entitled *Du pa rin po che gyud* relates that no material thing can have any reality. Its existence is relative to (our) wishes and desires. When attachment is withdrawn from them for the sake of attaining a state of (mental) vacuity (*Śūnyata*), it ceases to exist. When the mind comprehends relative existence and the illusory state of material things and refrains from clinging to them, it leads to the jñāna or knowledge of vacuity, the bright lustre of which, being devoid of anxiety and deliberation, encompasses all. This is the real object of meditation. Thus, by effecting a union of darśana and meditation, the attainment of emancipation is secured.

Nature of *Bonku* and *Bon Darśana*

The ninth volume of *Bon* aphorisms is said to agree with the theories of the *rDzogs chen pa* sect of the *rNying ma pa*. In *Bon* texts it is stated that the original basis-the purest nature which preceded both gShen, or the Buddha state, and *sattva*, or animal nature-is a vacuity called *Bonku*, which is the supreme ideal of the *Bon po*.

Bonku is not covered by the gloom of ignorance and desire. Nothing in itself, it is yet the source of consciousness in all. Existing from the beginning in the essence of the Buddha, it is not produced by the agency of *karma*. Being unconnected with the consequences of actions, it is self- existent, and it exists without effort. Its perception by the mind does not improve it, nor does the ignorance of it affect it in any way. It equally exists in the Buddha and in *sattva* without altering them for good or ill. This primaeval cause, which encompasses all, is the basis of all matter. All matter and transmigrating existences have emanated from it. All things are contained in it. Its action is diffused without obstruction. When the mind perceives it by well-regulated thinking, it acquires wisdom. If, however, it does not perceive it, it acquires *karma*, which is the cause of sin. If the meaning of the vacuity, the real basis, is investigated, the abode of time and space becomes evident. To reflection and well-regulated thinking it is fully manifest. From the conception of vacuity there emerge the three *Bon* images clearly. The soul is absorbed in the essence of *gShen*. The clearest lustre which is identified with *Bonku* or with the basis of all existence is self-existent. It is the nature of the Buddhas (*Bon saints*) and living beings. On account of non- discernment, it remains hidden from us. It is screened from us by the gloom of *avidyā*. When the supreme nature of the basis is uncovered, *Bonku* becomes manifest. No action of the mind or deliberation has anything to do with it. Then there arises wisdom. Simultaneously with the dawn of wisdom the thinking power is obstructed, and remembrance ceases. The mind, having lost its functions, becomes passive; it ceases to think. The position then may be compared to the instantaneous bliss of a sexual orgasm. The mind having ceased to form a conception of the supreme cause, Bonku emerges like an image on the mirror. This glorious lustre is called the self-born *jñāna* of *vidyā*. Undivided attention to it is called Bon darśana. In the region of the mind called *citta- rinchen*, which is immense and located in the eight petals of veins, there are five lustres of appearance belonging to the five organs of the body. In the middle of these five lustres sits *Bonku*, like a crystal ball, wrapped round by the thread of five jñānas. Its essence being vacuity, it is never perpetual. Nor, coming under the cognizance of *vidyā*, is it subject to annihilation. That this invisible essence exists in this manner must be learnt by meditation. Existing without cause and unseizable, it is pure in its nature.

Meditation (*sGom*)

Chos Kyi Nyima gives a detailed account of *Bon* meditation. According to this account the fully enlightened state of the mind, the continued and inseparable fixing of the mind on *Bonku*, is called *sGom*. It is of three kinds: (i) *Thun sgom*: This is performed by one who is initiated into it by a spiritual guide, i.e. by a lama. At first the mind does not remain absorbed in the particular object of meditation. At the second stage absorption and distraction are equal. At the last stage the mind enters upon a state of complete abstraction. Once perfect abstraction is achieved, it can be suspended, put off, or resumed at will. When the opportune time (time of attaining sainthood) comes, *sGom* reaches its utmost limit. (ii) *Nang sgom*: In its own time the mind gets filled with the light of *ātma-mukti-jñāna* and passes into deep meditation. It then becomes fully abstracted; so much so that it transcends meditation itself. Attainment of this state is the limit of *Nang sgom*. It can be compared to the calm and unruffled sea, the ideal of supreme inaction. (iii) *kLong sgom*: When, after acquiring all sorts of vidyā and seeing the objects aimed at, the mind has done with meditation and has ceased to think of the attainment of the essence of vacuity, it is time for *kLong sGom*. At this time all sins, all wicked thoughts, turn into wisdom; and all visible and invisible objects enter the all-pure region of *Bonku*. Transmigratory and emancipated existence, good and evil, mental attachment and separation, etc. are then seen to be without difference. A sublime state is attained. It is called *kLong sgom*.

According to Choi Kyi Nyima, these theories and notions of the *Bon po* bear a striking resemblance to those of the *rDzogs chen pa* sect of the *rNying ma pa* school. He also gives the Nine Vehicles of the *Bon* religion and their contents. His account is similar to the one given earlier.

He states that when the *Bon* religion was prospering, a synod of learned and erudite professors of *Bon* was held in the celebrated cavern of *gSan ba'i bon phug* in the *Mang mkhar* country. Priests and sages from China, India, sTag gzigs, and Tibet assembled there. A compendium of *Bon sge mo* or *sutras*, about 84,000 in number, was compiled. It is well known as *gSang sngags rdsong 'phrad nyi 'od rgyan.*

Monasteries and Bon Priests

Among *Bon* monasteries the gShen dar sding and gYung drung monasteries of rGyal mo rong were most notable. In later times, by the command of an emperor of China, most monasteries were pulled down, and a number of *Bon* religious establishments devastated. On the site of the gYung drung lHa sding monastery, a *dGe lugs pa* monastery called dGa' ldan was erected. An edict was issued, forbidding people to follow the *Bon* religion. And yet many *Bon* priests and monasteries managed to survive in rGyal rong, Tsho kha, Kong po, and other places. The Gon parituo monastery of Kham now has five hundred priests. Formerly the *Bon po* had no monastic system. Now, with the example of the Buddhists before them they have monks and nuns in their ranks. Some of these monks claim incarnate existence. In general, however, they are great drinkers of wine and eaters of meat. According to Choi Kyi Nyima, they are also not careful to avoid female company.

Nine Ways of Bon : An Assessment

The *Nine Ways of Bon* represent a succinct resume of the whole range of Tibetan religious practices: divining and predicting events, a practice to which Tibetans of all religious orders and of all ranks of society are addicted; the placating and repelling of local divinities of various kinds, of whose existence all Tibetans are equally convinced; the destruction of enemies by fierce *tantric* rites, a practice in which both the Buddhists and the Bon po are equally interested; the guiding of consciousness through the intermediate state, a power claimed equally by the older of Tibetan Buddhism and by the *Bon po;* moral discipline of devout believers and strict discipline of the monastic orders, a way of life that has followers in all religious orders in Tibet; *tantric* theories and rituals fundamental to the iconography and worship of all Tibetan religious communities; and tales of perfected wonder-working sages, which are typical again of the older orders of Tibetan Buddhism and of the *Bon po*. The Nine Ways, however, do not include the religious life of academic learning, which is now typical of educated monks of the *dGe lugs pa* or the Yellow Hat Sect. Perhaps at the time when the Nine Ways came into being, the *dGe* lugs pa way had not yet come into existence. Nowadays, however, the Bon po have this too, with their scholars of philosophy and logic and their academic honours and titles. They have in fact developed these diverse ways over the last thirteen centuries and produced a very large literature on their practices. Much of this literature - as, for example, some of their *sūtras* - is derived from the Buddhist. It would not be right to charge the *Bon po* with plagiarism as there was no conscious copying. They absorbed what was relevant and then retold it.[21]

It is not only the *Bon po* who have organized their doctrine into nine categories. The *rNying ma pa* too have done it. One must have imitated the other, but we cannot tell which of them came first. In fact the classification of all Buddhist teaching into nine *Theg pa* or Vehicles by the *rNying ma pa* is not accepted by the other orthodox Buddhist sects for fear that the *Bon po* system and beliefs might have influenced those of the *rNying ma pa* far too much. On the other hand a work entitled *lta ba'i rim pa* bshad pa attributed to a famous sage of the eighth century A.D., contains a short exposition of what the r*Nying ma pa* call the nine *Theg pa*. The authenticity of this work is not yet established. If this work is genuine, it would prove that the *Bon po* system is dependent on that of the *rNying ma pa.*[22]

21. Snellgrove, n.4, p.12.
22. Karmay, n.12, p.179.

CHAPTER FOUR

Bon Religion : Scriptures, Pantheon, Ritual

The *Bon po* canon[1] is, like the Buddhist, in two parts-the *bKa' 'gyur* and the *bStan 'gyur*. The *bKa' 'gyur* contains the discourses of gShen rab, and the *bStan 'gyur* consists of the commentaries, the rules of the order, rituals, and narratives and works connected with arts, logic, medicine, and poetry. The *Bon po* canon largely consists of two types of works.

Sources of the *Bon po* Canon

Gter ma or Rediscovered Texts: These are texts which were hidden during the period when the *Bon po* were under persecution in the eighth century. They were rediscovered in the tenth century and after. The earliest date of rediscovery is the year 913 A.D. according to *Bon po* tradition, but the codification of the *Bon po* texts took place when gShen chen klu dga (A.D. 996-1035) discovered a large number of texts in 1017 A.D.. His discovery makes up the main part of the *Bon po* canon. By the fourteenth century A.D. many more rediscoveries were made in various places. The texts were given different names; they were named after either the *gter ston* or the

1. Samten G.Karmay, *A General Introduction to the History and Doctrines of Bon* (Tokyo, 1975), pp. 188-91.

rediscoverers or the places where they were rediscovered. There is, however, a controversy over their authenticity. Orthodox Buddhists call *gter ma* apocryphal. Many Western scholars are inclined to agree with them. However, not all religious texts belonging to this category are of doubtful authenticity. Rediscovery of texts is not unique to Bon *po* tradition. The literature of the *rNying ma pa,* the older sect of Buddhism in Tibet, is full of rediscovered texts. Many of those who rediscovered texts were simple, ordinary people. *Bon po* historians do not claim that any miraculous power was used to rediscover texts. For instance, in the tenth century three Nepalese wanderers found *Bon po* texts in the bSam yas monastery by accident. As they were not interested in them they exchanged them for food. In the same century three hunters come across *Bon po* texts when they were digging in the ground for stone. In the twelfth century a shepherd happened to walk into a cave and found that the cave was full of books. Similarly several pilgrims and travellers found texts in old temples, stupas, and statues. Several of those who rediscovered texts belonged to both the *Bon po* and *rNying ma pa* traditions. There are a number of instances where a *Bon po gter ston* found a Buddhist text and handed it over to a follower of the *rNying ma pa* and vice versa. These examples establish that it was common for Tibetans to find texts by accident in the most unexpected places. However, since only a few native Tibetan works can definitely be assigned to the eighth century A.D., it is clear that many of the *gter ston* who found old manuscripts used them as a basis and then rewrote or expanded the originals. For example, *gZer myig* which was rediscovered by Drang rje btsun pa, contains material which has parallel versions in the Tung huang manuscripts.

Orally Transmitted Texts : sNyan rgynd

There are two kinds of orally transmitted texts. According to *Bon po* tradition, one who "receives" such texts is normally considered to have had a close spiritual connexion with the teacher concerned. The teacher and the disciple were not contemporaries. The teacher lived several centuries before. He appeared later in a vision to his disciple and dictated his teaching to him. The disciple wrote down what he heard. It is explained that the teacher who lived in the eighth century A.D. "concealed" the texts in his mind during the time of persecution. That is to say, he memorized the texts before they were destroyed. When the right time came to reveal the teaching, he recited the texts to a person whom he recognized as his own spiritual son. While the *gter ston* found manuscripts on which they based their works, the recipients of oral transmission never claimed to have found anything for them to produce such bulky volumes as *gZi brjid*, the longest version of gShen rab's life, without any basis.

There is another type of oral transmission. This is considered to be a genuine oral transmission as we have a long list of historical persons through whom the oral preceptual teaching has been transmitted. *Zhang Zhung snyan rgyud* belongs to this category.

By the beginning of the fifteenth century A.D., the *Bon po* had put out numerous works of both the *gter ma* and *snyan rgyud* traditions. The assembly of the canon was, however, undertaken in a very selective manner. The systematic collection, codification, and actual editing took place only in the middle of the eighteenth century in the rGyal rong monastery, i.e. after that of the Buddhist *bKa' 'gyur* and the *bStan 'gyur* which had been completed in the early thirteenth century A.D., in the monastery at sNar thang. Manuscript editions of the canon are said to exist at least in twentyeight *Bon po* monasteries in Tibet, mostly in Hor and Khyung po. When Tibetan refugees started pouring into India in 1959, the Bon po monk, Sangs rgyas bstan 'dzin, carried with him a very detailed catalogue (*dkar chag*) of the *Bon po* canon. This catalogue was made by the famous twentysecond abbot of the sMan ri monastery, Nyima bstan 'dzin (b.1813 A.D.). According to this catalogue, there are 113 volumes of the *bKa 'gyur* and 293 of the *bKa' brten; bKa'* are the word of gShen rab, and *bka' brten* are works that depend on the *bKa'*.

We have already spoken about the classification of the teaching of gShen rab into Four Portals and one Treasury. The catalogue prepared by Nyima bstan 'dzin classifies the works of gShen rab into four divisions according to his orders. These four divisions are: (i) Vols 1 to 46 of *mDo*, which consist of texts dealing in the main with monastic discipline, cosmogony, hagiographical literature, and prayers; (ii) Vols 47 to 66 of *'Bum*, which contain mainly the *Bon po Prajñāpāramitā* literature; (iii) Vols 67 to 107 of *rGyud*, which contain mainly *Bon po* esoteric teaching; and (iv) Vols 108 to 113 of mDzod, which comprise *Bon po rDzogs chen* philosophy.

The *'Bum* division is in fact a wholesale borrowing of the Buddhist *Prajñāpāramitā*. The *mDo* and *rGyud* divisions respectively correspond to the Buddhist terms "*sutra*" and "*tantra*". The *mDzod* does not have any connexion with *Abhidharmakośa* but has a certain affiliation to the *rDzogs chen* of the *rNying ma pa*.

The *bKa' brten* part of the canon, which consists of 293 volumes, deals with rituals, narratives, and commentaries of all kinds, and works connected with arts, logic, medicine, and poetry.

rDzogs chen

rDzogs chen ("Great Achievement") is as important a part of *Bon po* tradition as it is of Tibetan Buddhism. It is regarded as the highest among the nine *Theg pa* of the *Bon po*. In the *rNying ma pa* system it is known as *Ati Yoga - rTsol sgrub dang bral ba'i theg pa.*

According to *rNying ma pa* tradition, it was the Tibetan monk Vairocana who introduced the *rDzogs chen* teaching into Tibet in the eighth century A.D., It is considered to be a teaching exceeding all else. It is held that it can bring about the realization of Buddhahood in the present life itself. However, some orthodox Buddhists believe that it is of Chinese origin. They, further, believe that it was brought to Tibet by Hva shang Mahayana and that it was proved to be false in the debate between Indian and Chinese scholars at the court of King Khri srong lde brtsan. (The Indian side was represented by Sāntārakśitā). *rDzogs chen* has consequently been a controversial subject. Most people are now inclined to hold that, although in *rDzogs chen* there may be ideas and practices parallel to those of the Chinese, it is clearly of Indo-Tibetan origin.

In *Bon po* tradition the word "*rDzogs chen*" covers three systems of meditation. The first system is *A-khrid,* taught by the hermit dGangs.mdzod (1030-96 A.D.). The second is *rDzogs chen*, introduced by the *gter ston* bZhod ston dngos grub grags pa, when he rediscovered a group of texts called *rDzogs chen yang rtse klong chen* in 1088 A.D.. This system corresponds to the Buddhist tradition of *sems sde*. It is, therefore, directly related to the *rDzogs chen* of the *rNying ma pa.* Last, we have Shang Zhung *snyan* rgyud, considered to be the most important of all

2. Ibid., pp. 213-15.

the systems of meditation among the *Bon po*. Shang shung *snyan rgyud* is said to derive from the Shang shung master Gyer spungs sNang bzher lod po in the eighth century A.D.. One of its distinctive features is the belief in the five lights of five different colours and in the *kun gzhi*, or the primordial intelligence as the begetter of the state of either ignorance or enlightenment.[3]

Origin of the World[4]

According to the *Bon* religion, the world emerged from several eggs, but there are many versions, and there is no universally accepted account. A *Bon po* ritual normally begins with a narrative on the emergence of the gods and the demons into existence. The narrative is different almost every time, even about the same god or demon. However, a general pattern can be worked out from the scattered and diverse accounts contained in the *Bon po* text Srid pa'i mdzod phug (considered to be *bKa'*, the word of gShen rab, and hence part of the *Bon po* canon). The story of the creation is broadly as follows:

> In the beginning of the beginning there was the Lord Nam mkha' stong ldan phyod sum, who possessed the lees of the five causes. The father, Khri rgyal khug pa, collected them to his body and softly uttered the syllable "Ha". From this utterance sprang wind. As the wind circled fast in the form of a wheel of light, fire arose. The faster the wind blew, the hotter the fire grew. Dew was produced from the heat of the fire and the coolness of the wind. On drops of dew were clusters of atoms. These in turn were stirred by the wind, which travelled about in space causing accumulations of particles to grow to the size of mountains. The world was in this way created by the father, Khri rgyal khug pa (allias mNgon rdzogs rgyal po).

3. Ibid.
4. Ibid., pp.191-6.

From the essence of the five causes two eggs emerged---an egg of light and an egg of darkness. The gods came out of the egg of light. Srid pa sangs po 'bum khri arose from the heart of the egg. Srid pa sangs po 'bum khri in time became king of the world of existence. The egg of darkness was the home of ignorance, fog, torpor, and madness. From the core of it was born Mun pa zer ldan nag po, the king of non-existence. These two, Srid pa sangs po 'bum khri and Mun pa zer ldan nag po, were the progenitors of the gods and the demons respectively.

The five causes produced dew and rain, which in course of time became the oceans. With the blowing of the wind a bubble the size of a tent surfaced, containing a blue egg of light. From this blue egg there appeared a blue woman. Srid pa sangs po 'bum khri named her Chu lcan rgyal mo. The blue woman produced wild animals, birds, and beasts together with nine brothers and nine sisters. The father assigned a particular role to each one of them.

The nine brothers caused nine women to appear and to become their wives, and the nine sisters created nine men and chose them as their husbands. From them came all living beings. The parents and the eighteen offspring constitute the original ancestors of the *Bon po* gods. Most of the gods in *Bon* and Tibetan Lamaism whose origin is not Indian can be traced back to this mythological event.

The god of darkness, Mun pa zer ldan nag po, created sTong zhams nag mo out of his own shadow. He then made her his queen. Out of their union eight brothers and eight sisters were born. These created their own male and female partners. Thus arose the *Bon po* world of demons.

The idea of eggs as the primaeval source of gods and demons is quite unique to *Bon* in Tibet. *Bon po* tradition gives no indication of time, but it does assign an important role to space in the world's creation, its personification being Nam mkha 'stong ldan phyod sum rje who is invisible and passive. Subsequently he was stylized as *Bon sku* which corresponds to Chos sku or Dharamakaya in Buddhism. The visible and active god is Khri rgyal khug pa, also called mGon rdzogs rgyal po, the king who possesses clarity. He is the same as gShen lha 'od dkar. He is stylised as *Longs sku*, or *Sambhogakaya* in Buddhism. To these two figures gShen rab mi bo is added as the guide of all living beings, thus forming the *Bon po* triad.

The idea of creation of the world in *Bon po* tradition is not the same as it is in Christianity and Islam. The Christians and the Muslims believe that God created the world out of nothing. The idea of omnipotence does not exist in *Bon po* tradition. It is not a myth of creation. Rather it is one of procreation.

There are four heavens in *Bon po* tradition. They are called *gNas rigs chen po bzhi* or the Four Great Residences. They are for the use of the gods, according to their different requirements, such as discussion before taking important decisions, purification before descending to the earth or after returning from the earth, education, etc. The demons live in the north. This is in line with ideas in the religious system of sTag gzigs. The influence of sTag gzigs is clear in the *Bon* belief in duality. Duality such as light and darkness, white and black, good and evil, gods and demons, the worlds of existence and non-existence, creation and destruction, etc. forms one of the fundamental tenets of the *Bon* religion. Any ritual or ceremony performed by the *Bon po* has this angle of duality. The gods should triumph over the demons, and the good should prevail over the evil.

Man is closely connected with the gods, but he should take care not to give offence to the gods or to the spirits of evil. In difficulties he can seek the help of the gods who must necessarily triumph over their adversaries. However, the gods and the demons are not separate. They only represent opposing forces, and both these forces are present in man. Man's actions are determined by those external forces, not by internal ones. When Buddhism came, this idea gradually merged in the idea of *karma* and later in the idea of innate intelligence and ignorance derived from the *rDzogs chen* philosophy. It would appear that the *Bon* religion received these influences very early when Shang shung was still an independent state. Although Buddhist teaching in *mDzod phug* outweighs the influence of *Bon*, the bilingual, archaic composition on the cosmological origin of the world is very ancient. The work represents a typical synthesis of *Bon* and Buddhism.

Bon po Pantheon

The *Bon po* pantheon[5] consists of a large number of gods whose origin can invariably be traced to Shang shung, India, China, sTag gzigs, and Tibet itself. Though the entire range of these gods is not available in an organized form, the *Bon po* have collections of small groups of divinities. Each group of such divinities calls for a different kind of ritual. The divinities are represented on *thang kas*, miniature cards called *tsa ka li*, blocks of wood, and wall paintings. In fact images, *thang kas*, and wall paintings of individual deities may be found

5. Ibid., pp. 196-202.

everywhere among the *Bon po*. According to the original genealogy of the *Bon po* gods as given in *mDzod phug*, there is a systematized structure to which they all relate. For instance, the four principal deities, described as the tranquil deities (*Zhi bai lha*) and mentioned in *gZer myig* as the chief ones, are : (1) Sa trig er sangs; (2) gShen lha 'od dkar; (3) Sangs po 'bum khri; and (4) gShen rab mi bo.

The last three constitute the *Bon po* triad. gShen lha 'od dkar is the same as Khri rgyal khug pa, the primaeval god. While Sangs po 'bum khri is the primary father of gods, the others belong to the mythology of creation. In the triad, gShen lha is the teacher, and Sangs po is companion to gShen rab and is looked upon as the guide and saviour of this world. The first of the four, Sa trig er sangs, is another name for the primary mother of beings, Chu lcan rgyal mo. She is the Great Mother of Deities (*yum chen*). Her function as one of the four tranquil deities corresponds to that of *Prajñā* in Buddhism as the Mother of all the Buddhas.

The five main terrifying divinities are known as *gSas mkhan mchog lnga,* the Excellent Ones of the *gSas Citadel*. The first three of these are (1) dBal gsas rngam pa; (2) lHa rgod thog pa; and (3) gTso mchog mkha' 'gying. They are known as the triple tantric divinities of the *Bon po* pantheon. Iconographically, they resemble those of the Buddhist pantheon. Their origin, however, is not Indian. In fact it goes back to the original *Bon po* genealogy.

The fourth divinity in this category is *Ge khod,* originally a mountain god residing on Mount *Ti se* and, therefore, of Shang shung origin. Mythologically he is said to have descended from the heavens in the form of a yak and then disappeared into the mountains. Gradually this god rose in status and became a *yi dam*, a tutelary divinity in the *Bon po* pantheon. He has been a terrifying divinity since then, with multiple heads and arms, and he is generally represented as embracing his consort in *yab yum*. He has three hundred and sixty subordinate divinities. He has much to do with the astrological and divination gods.

The fifth divinity belonging to this group of gods is *Phur pa*. This deity is worshipped not only by the *Bon po*, but also by the *rNying ma pa* and *Sa skya pa* sects of Buddhism. The origin of this deity is, perhaps, Indian. According to *rNying ma pa*, he was introduced into the Tibetan pantheon by the saint Padmasambhava. This, however, is controversial. There are today many variations of the cult of *Phur pa*. The object of propitiating *Phur pa* is to force an opponent into submission.

Besides the *yi dam* there are many *Bon po* gods who are religious guardians. They are called *bKa' skyong,* the protectors of the word of gShen rab mi bo. Further it was a common practice in Tibet in the days of old to deify the spirits of well-known people and make them religious protectors. The abbots of some of the famous monasteries as well as well-known monks belong to this category.

Bon po Rituals

The ritual[6] in the Bon religion are quite rich in quality and variety. They are considered extremely important for understanding the working of the human mind in ancient times. All rituals are grouped in the first four of the Nine Ways (*Theg pa*) of *Bon* : (1) The Way of gShen of prediction; (2) the Way of gShen of the visual world; (3) the Way of gShen of existence; and (4) the

6. Ibid., pp. 202-7.

Way of gShen of illusion. The first is subdivided into four categories : (1) *mo* (divination); (2) *rtsis* (astrology); (3) *gto* (rites); and (4) *dpyad* (diagnoses).

Each rite is accompanied by a narrative. The narrative is a mythological account of a certain event that took place in the beginning of the world. It is narrated in order to recreate the necessary atmosphere. In the narrative the priests assert that they are the followers of their forefathers and that, therefore, they are as effective as their forefathers in calling on gods or in exorcising demons. The narrative usually has a connexion with the original genealogy and is a means to justify the action that the priests take in the course of the rite. There are many everyday rites, the principal ones being those relating to the performance of marriages and invocation of divine aid in ensuring long life and the continuance of the line, increase of wealth, augmentation of good fortune, and the warding off of misfortune as well as prayers for good harvests and the peace of the dead. Four simultaneous stages are involved in the carrying out of a rite. For example, if someone is ill, he first goes to the diviner (*mo ba*) who consults his divination manual to see whether the patient is afflicted by any malignant spirit (*gdon*). If such a spirit is involved, he advises on the kind of rite to be carried out to pacify that spirit. The patient then goes to an astrologer (*rtsis pa*). The astrologer examines whether the patient's birth star and the planets are in order and whether the favourable and adverse elements connected with his birth star have come into conflict. He then recommends a date on which the rite should take place. While those consultations are in progress, the patient is referred to a physician for a diagnosis (*dpyad*) of his illness. This method is used to cover all the everyday problems of ordinary people. It is in fact considered to be one of the essential practices of the *Bon* religion. The rites are probably quite effective at the psychological level; the diagnosis by the physician takes care of the physical aspect.

Each rite begins with purification. The process of purification consists of three parts : (1) The removal of the poison (*dug phyung*); (2) purification through the sprinkling of water; and (3) purification by fumigation.

Removal of Poison

As we have seen, there are two kinds of forces, the gods and the demons. Poison comes from the latter. There are several kinds of poison. Poison can grow out of the earth; it can be found in certain kinds of stone (some sort of pyrites); it can ooze out of trees, shrubs, etc. Some poisonous substances are burnt in a small ladle before the purificatory rite begins. The fumes are then allowed to spread to all parts of the house. Meanwhile the priests participating in the rite start chanting. The idea is that if any poison is lurking in the vicinity, the process of purification cannot be effective.

Purification of Pollution

Many kinds of pollution are mentioned in the *Bon po* texts. Some of them are considered to be more serious like consumption of the flesh of a horse, a human corpse, sexual intercourse with a woman who has commited a murder, and the use of the clothes of a murderer by another. One must purify oneself both physically and spiritually.

First, the physical purification. One method is to mix the juices of certain medicinal plants and the water of lakes and of mountain snow (particularly the water of the lake *Ma pham* and the snow of Mount *Ti se*) and to sprinkle the mixture on the man concerned. Another method is fumigation. A number of fresh plants are gathered and burnt in a little ladle with a long handle. If it is outside the house, a high platform is specially built for the purpose. As many of the plants are difficult to get in certain regions, *juniper* and *mkhan pa* are commonly burnt. These two are sometimes referred to as *gyu lo* ("turquoise leaves") and *gser lo* ("golden leaves"). The juniper tree is the *Bon po* sacred tree. It is often called *lHa shing shug pa gyu* lo ("tree of the gods"). Its fragrant smoke is believed to have the effect of purifying any pollution that one may have suffered. It is also offered to the mountain gods. The word "*bsang*" used in the sense of offering is the same as in the purificatory rite. The narratives relating to the purificatory rite speak of a medicinal bird, the white grouse. The use of its patterned feathers reminds one of the peacock in Indian mythology, which is believed to be capable of destroying poison. The feathers of the white grouse are used to sprinkle the water of purification in Buddhist ceremonies even today. The use of peacock feathers was adopted by the *Bon po* in later centuries.

Marriage Rites

Bon po marriage rites are most interesting.[7] They differ from one region to another. Nobody has made a proper study of them so far. Marriage is such a common, earthly institution that Buddhism has not formulated any fundamental doctrine about it. Tibetan Buddhism did devise marriage rites now and then along the lines of *Bon po* ceremonial rites whenever lay devotees requested them. These rites were not uniform in character. There is an

7. Ibid., pp. 207-13.

interesting account written by Kong sprul yon tan rgya mtsho (1813-99 A.D.), on the occasion of the marriage of a prince of *Derge* to a daughter of mDo mkhar ba in *dBus*. He organized the ceremonies into seven parts within the framework of *Bon po* ritual incorporating Buddhist divinities and using some parts of Indian mythology. As he was originally a *Bon po* he was well acquainted with their marriage rites. According to this work the marriage rites are divided as follows: (1) the exorcising of the spirits that might come ahead of the bride; (2) the purification of the bride so that nothing might pollute the god of the hearth; (3) the spreading of the carpet for the bride; (4) the offering of the three white foods to the bride; (5) the giving of a new name to the bride; (6) invoking of the gods for protection; (7) the summoning of the *gyang*; and (8) prayers.

On the one hand it omits the myths and legends associated with *Bon po* rites; on the other it includes certain ceremonies not in vogue among the *Bon po*.

For a *Bon po* ceremony of marriage no temple or public building is required. There is no customary registration. Occasionally a marriage contract is drawn up. This is sealed by the two houses concerned, each house retaining a copy. Before the actual marriage a rite called *Glang chen san bsgyur* is performed when the bride approaches the house of the bridegroom. Details of this ceremony are, however, not available. As for the actual marriage, there are several versions. One of them is entitled *Ming sring dpal bgos dang lha 'dogs*, and it is in two parts: *Ming sring dpal bgos* (the dividing of the wealth between the brother and the sister) and *lha 'dogs* (entrusting to the gods). The first part is a mythical account of the first marriage of a man to a goddess. Here is an account of it in summary form:

The god Zom 'brang (alias Sangs po 'bum khri) and his wife Gung btsun ma (alias Chu lcan rgyal mo) had a daughter named Srid lcan 'phrul mo che and a son called lHa sras Ijon pa (alias Srid rje 'brang dkar). As the goddess was very beautiful, there were many wanting to marry her. One of the men called Ling dkar, the Lord of *rGya*, asked her father for her hand in marriage. The god replied : "My daughter would go from the gods to the gods and is not made for any black-headed man. Just as the sun and the moon do not fall from the sky to the earth, the gods in the sky would not come down to the earth." At this, the man said : "I want to take a wife of good origin. I am of the race of man of the spacious earth, the head of the line from whom man will multiply. If men and the gods come together, the men will worship the gods, and the gods will protect the men; they would be kind to each other. Although the sun and the moon shine in the sky, their rays come to the earth. The warm vapour that the earth exudes goes up into the sky and becomes a cloud. This is an example of what we are to each other. Thus give me your daughter in marriage." After some further argument the Lord of the gods was convinced and gave his consent to the marriage. He demanded as bride- price various things such as gold, turquoise, garments, and an arrow and animals like horses and sheep. These were to be brought to the land of the gods by the seven *gNye'u* (Kinsmen of the groom). This done, the time of departure of the bride arrived. Before departing, the bride and her brother played dice for their share in the inheritance from their parents. The game was played under the supervision of the priest lHa bon thod dkar. The bride claimed half the property, but as she was only a girl, she was able to get just one-third of it. The brother invoked the gods, saying : "I play the dice of *Pho lha* from the right, I play the dice of *sGra bla* from the left, I play the dice of the *Srog lha* in front, I play the dice of *Yul lha* behind. I play the dice of being heir to my father." He won a large share. The sister then scattered seven grains of blue barley to the sky, and said: "If I have a god, may he protect me today. *Ma lha*, play the heavenly dice. *sGra bla gnyen po,* be a witness unto this." She played the dice which came up single.

When she left, her father gave her an arrow as a parting gift. The mother gave her a spindle, and the brother a turquoise. She offered her salutations to the gods, to the priest, to her parents, and to her brother. Then, attaching a roll of white silk to the right-hand side of the lap of the bride, the seven *gÑye'u* led her away to the land of men. At the same time the priest lHa bon thod dkar performed the rite of *gyang gugs* at the house of the Lord of the gods.

A word about the significance of this ceremony. This rite *gyang 'gugs* means "the summoning of the essence of fortune". It is important because, if a bride leaves her father's house for good, the *gyang* of the family might also depart. This is considered to be unlucky for the family. A similar rite takes place at the house of the groom. This is auspicious because the bride comes in with her wealth and opens up the prospect of the continuance of the family line. "*Gyang*" connotes an abstract idea rather than any tangible object. It is the idea of symbolic wealth. It is also used in several other senses - as, for example, in such expressions as "*rGya gar chos gyang*" (the *gyang* of the religion from India), "sTag gzigs *nor gyang*" (The gyang of the wealth of stag gzigs), or simply "rta gyang" ("the *gyang* of the horse"). In Amdo it is a common practice for the owner to pull out a few hairs from the mane of his horse about to be sold and attach it to the door of the enclosure where his horses are kept. It is a symbolic gesture to retain the *gyang* of the horse even though it may be sold at a good price. If a good horse is lost or dies, it is described as "*gyang shor ba*" ("the .scape of the "gyang"). Hence the imperative need to perform the rite of *gyang 'gugs*. The word "*gyang*" very often occurs with "*phyva*". And then the expression denotes life. The word "*gyang*" is also used with reference to sheep as an epithet - *gyang mo lug*. Among the *Bon po* the sheep are a symbol of *gyang* because of their usefulness for the maintenance of human life. According to a legend the first sheep came into existence when Srid pa ye smon rgyal po wished to have something that would supply the essential needs of man. This first sheep is called *Lug lha ba bal' chen;* it is the god of sheep.

In the second part of the marriage rite, *lha 'dogs,* a thread made of wool called *dmu thag* is attached to the lap of the groom, and a blue thread called *gyang thag* is attached to the lap of the bride. The groom holds an arrow and makes offerings of *chang* and *gtor ma* to the five gods of the head; and the bride holds a spindle and makes offerings of curd and *phye mar* ("mixture of *rtsam pa* and butter"). The priest presents the groom with a gold ornament (either a ring or an ear-ring) called *bla gser* ("the soul-gold"). He also presents the bride with a turquoise *bla gyu* ("the soul - turquoise"). The couple are seated on a white felt carpet on which a *swastika* of barley grain is laid. The priest then begins the rite, chanting together with the couple.

The chanting is about the original genealogy of the world, followed by a story about the original source of the arrow, the spindle, and the material of the *dmu thag* and the *gyang thag*.

This serves also as the rite of *gyang 'gugs*. The arrow is the symbol of man while the spindle is that of woman. The dmu thag was connected with the early Tibetan kings. It was in the form of light, and whenever a king died, his body dissolved gradually into light from feet upwards. This light then joined with the *dmu thag* which dissolved into the heaven of *dMu*. The place of origin of Tibetan kings is sometimes *dMu* and sometimes

Phyva. According to a legend a messenger of *Phyva* goes to the heaven of *dMu*, asking for a *dMu* king to rule over black-headed men.

The story of the arrow, the spindle, the dmu thag, and the *gyang* thag is as follows: Up there in the valley there was the father Phyva gang gyang grags. The mother was Srid pa'i glong bsang ma. From their union three heavenly eggs came into existence. Following the bursting of the golden egg a golden arrow with turquoise tail feathers appeared. This was the arrow of life. Following the bursting of the turquoise egg a turquoise arrow with golden tail feathers appeared. This was the glorious arrow of the bride. Following the bursting of the conch-white egg a gold spindle came into existence. From out of the light rays of the sky and the vapour of the ocean a white clump of *Bon* came into existence. This was drawn out and spun by the wind. It was wound round a tree. The name that was given to this yarn was *dMu thag* and *gyang thag.*

Towards the end, the chanting says that the man and the woman are entrusted to the gods. Though they have been born and have matured separately they will now be united as one. The life of the bride and the bridegroom depends on this unity. They are entrusted to the gods to lead a happy life hereafter.

Apart from being a weapon, the arrow plays an important role as the symbol of man in legends as well as in actual life. There are three kinds of arrows in the marriage rite. The first is *lHa mda' sgro dkar*, the divine arrow with white tail feathers which is the *rten* ("support") of the five gods of the head. This is part of the bride-price brought by the seven *gNye'u*. Next there is *Tshe mda' nya mig,* the life arrow, the groom's arrow, the symbol of man. The third is *dpal mda'*, the glorious arrow, given as a parting gift to the bride by her father. The use of this arrow is not clear. However, in some regions in Tibet an arrow is attached to the collar of the bride when she sets out from her home to the bridegroom's house. The use of this arrow thus varies as much as the marriage custom. In Amdo District every male member of a family in a *Bon po* home possesses an arrow which is about two feet long and decorated completely with five pieces of silk of different colours, a silver mirror, and a turquoise. An arrow is brought by the maternal uncle when a son is born. This is kept in the family chapel. This practice is in accordance with the texts relating to the marriage rite, and indicates that when the wife gives birth to a son, an arrow must be planted on the pillow and that, when a girl is born, it should be a spindle.

Another custom is for a man to plant an arrow (*mda' rgod*) in a cairn (*la btsas*) situated on the shoulder of a mountain nearby. This is followed by a great feast and offering of juniper *bsang* to the *Yul lha* to whom the arrow is entrusted. The arrow planted in the cairn may be from ten to fifteen feet long. In the place of tail feathers, three wooden painted slats are made in the shape of feathers and attached to the tail of the shaft. On this arrow silk of five different colours is not attached. Instead one finds a *rlung rta*, the symbol of fortune. It is a piece of cloth printed with prayers from the *gyang 'gugs* rite. The colour of one's own *rlung rta*, is in accordance with the element in one's horoscope so that the *rlung rta* of each person is one of the five colours.

The arrow is particularly important for the opening up of the marriage relationship. The expression in Tibetan for this is "*gnyen lam mda' yis phye ba*", which means that the way of the marriage relationship is to be opened by the arrow. Another related expression is "*gnyen lam dar gyis shrel ba*" which means that the way of the marriage relationship is to be connected by silk. This is in accordance with the legend, which says that the goddess was led away after attaching a roll of silk to her lap. According to another legend, the minister mGar stong btsan yul zung took an arrow when he went to China to ask for the hand of the Chinese princess for King Srong brtsan sgam po. The Emperor presented him with three hundred girls of the same age and told him to select his daughter from among them. The minister, thereupon, presented the arrow to the princess. According to a legend, an arrow was also demanded by the *dMu* when the messengers of *Phyva* asked the gods for a king. This means that the opening up of relationships through an arrow is not necessarily confined to marriage.

Persecution of the *Bon po* in the Eighth Century and Subsequent Developments

Buddhism was introduced into Tibet in the reign of King Srong brtsan sgam po. A literary language was also introduced, and foreign religious literature was eytensively translated into that language. The practice of keeping records too began. The motive of the king in introducing Buddhism into Tibet were political rather than religious. It would appear that he wanted his country to acquire sophistication through cultural intercourse with the neighbouring civilizations. Simultaneously he was loyal to his ancestral religion, *Bon*, in which the king was regarded as a divine being.[8] In the beginning Buddhism adopted a conciliatory approach to secure Royal indulgence and protection for its practice. And it served to increase Royal power.

8. David L.Snellgrove and Hugh E.Richardson, *A Cultural History of Tibet* (Boulder, Colo., 1980), p.28.

Though not neglected by the rulers, *Bon* found that it could not rival the more sophisticated philosophical structure of Buddhism. It, therefore, started developing its own doctrines and a philosophy on Buddhist lines. In this effort it was aided by the conservative group of ministers who felt that their privileges were being threatened by the new religion. Thus there ensued a keen struggle between Buddhism and *Bon*. In fact the thirst of the nobles for political power was often disguised by religious disputations; so much so that a rival faction of nobles managed to get Buddhism banned in Tibet when King Khri srong lde brtsan was a minnor.

By this time Tibet was one unified state, following conquests by Srong brtsan sgam po. Shang shung, considered to be the home of *Bon*, was annexed to Tibet; its culture and religion were absorbed. Gradually *Bon* was able to challenge the foreign religion, viz Buddhism. With the establishment of the bSam yas monastery in the reign of Khri srong lde brtsan, the fourth successor of Srong brtsan sgam po, and its consecration by Guru Padmasambhava, it was clear that Buddhism had triumphed. It was, however, a political rather than a purely religious success. Ancient beliefs were so deeply embedded in the Tibetan psyche that the masses still followed *Bon*. The King was sympathetically inclined towards Buddhism. He allowed both religions to coexist. He favoured now this religion and now that. Friction between the two religions continued. One particular instance of friction was the offering of bloody sacrifices by the *Bon po*. The Buddhists did not like it. They brought the sacrifices to the notice of the King, protesting eloquently that Buddhism could not countenance them. The King counselled patience; he was compelled to take cognizance of the views of the Tibetan nobility and the

Bon po.[9] When he felt that he was strong enough to have hiw own way, he organized a debate. It is said that Buddhist scholars were able to defeat the *Bon po* convincingly. This enabled the King to do away with *Bon*. He started persecuting the *Bon po*. He called all *Bon* priests together and gave them the choice of becoming Buddhist monks or tax-paying citizens. If neither of the two alternatives was acceptable, they should leave the country. The King is reported to have upbraided the priests in the following words which were clearly directed towards the Tibetan nobles as well : "As the *Bon po* are strong, I suspect that you are trying to wean my subjects away from me." He forbade animal sacrifice. He also threatened to put to death those who had turned Buddhist texts into *Bon* texts by subtle alterations. Many of the smaller shrines of the *Bon po* are reported to have been destroyed and the others taken over by the Buddhists.[10]

One result was that many *Bon po* publicily went over to Buddhism. The greater number, however, preferred exile. They hid their holy writings wherever they felt they were not likely to be discovered by the King's men - in the mountains, in the ravines, and even in the monasteries of unsuspecting Buddhist monks. The idea was to save those writings for the benefit of future generations. In later centuries the rediscovery of these literary treasures played an important role in assembling the *Bon po* canon. The much-venerated *Bon po* sage, Dran pa nam mkha, was one of those who consented to embrace Buddhism. In this way, according to *Bon po* tradition, the adherents of *Bon* tried to save their religion from being eradicated.[11]

---

9. Helmut Hoffman, *The Religions of Tibet,* Edward Fitzgerald, trans. (London, 1961), edn 2, pp.72-74.
10. Ibid., pp.78-82.
11. Karmay, n.1, pp.183-6.

King Khri srong lde brtsan thus failed to destroy the *Bon* religion altogether. In view of the repressive measures he took, the *Bon po* led an isolated life, away from the mainstream of the country's spiritual pursuits. And yet they kept up their struggle: they still had the support of powerful Tibetan nobles. The conflict remained more or less underground during the rest of the reign of Khri srong, as also during the subsequent two reigns, viz the reign of Mu ne brtsan po (797-98 A.D.), and that of Sad nam legs (798-817 A.D.), Many of those who went over to Buddhism remained *Bon po* at heart : only their bodies and their tongues practised Buddhism. On the other hand nothing changed in the traditional leaning of the Royal house towards Buddhism. The Kings encouraged Buddhists more and more and strengthened Buddhist priesthood.[12]

The power of the Buddhist priests reached its zenith in the reign of King Ral pa can (817-36 A.D.). This King supported in particular the literary efforts of the Buddhist priests. He left nothing undone to further their interests, to strengthen their position, and to afford them personal advantage. His feeling of veneration towards them was legendary. The real power of the State increasingly passed into the hands of the Buddhists, and their influence was more flaunted in public life than was tolerable to Tibetan national pride.[13] The common people, as well as the nobles, were compelled to conform to Buddhist standards of morality. In the end popular indignation burst out in violent anti-clerical demonstrations. The King supported the Buddhist priesthood and severely punished anyone guilty of any offence against the Buddhists. There were

12. Hoffman, n.9, p.80.
13. Ibid.

even instances of inhuman punishment like the cutting off of fingers or the putting out of eyes. This led to a conspiracy by the nobles who sympathized with the *Bon po*, and they had the King assassinated.

The victorious conspirators put a new King on the throne--- gŁang dar ma (836-42 A.D.). This King leaned towards the nobles and the *Bon po*; so much so that the opposite of what happened under Ral pa can took place under his rule. He launched a policy of brutal repression of Buddhism which did not even spare Buddhist literature. Many valuable texts were either burnt or thrown into water. As a consequence a fanatic Buddhist monk, dPal gyi rdo rje, killed the King with an arrow when the King was reading an inscription on one of the obelisks set up in Lhasa. He later claimed that he had acted "out of compassion" to prevent the King from committing further crimes and had thus helped him to attain a better rebirth.[14]

The consequences of these religious and political upheavals were negative. The religious confusion and the struggle between the monarch and the nobles weakened the country beyond limits. The country disintegrated politically and broke up before long into numerous small principalities. The authority of the Central Government was limited to the capital. The collapse was complete not only politically but also culturally. Both religions - Buddhism and *Bon* - suffered grievous blows, and, for almost a century and a half thereafter, practically nothing is known about Tibet. This period of Tibetan history is known as the Dark Age of Tibet.[15]

---

14. Ibid., p.82.
15. Ibid.,p.83.

Revival

It was with the rediscovery of certain *Bon* texts by gShen chen klu dga' in 1017 A.D., that a renewed "propagation of Bon" began. These rediscovered texts formed the nucleus of the *Bon po* canon. gShen chen klu dga is one of the most important names in the later development of *Bon*. In fact, with him, *Bon* emerged as a fully organized religion. It became more or less a form of Buddhism, but without giving up its own characteristic doctrines and practices. The *Bon po* adopted at this time a policy of reconciliation towards Buddhism. They accepted the Buddha as an emanation of gShen rab and as one of the six divinities who guided sentient beings from the six kinds of existence. They also embraced all the beliefs and practices that were available in Tibet without caring for their sources. In other words, *Bon* embraced all the religions of Tibet and represented Tibetan Lamaism in its fullest sense.[16]

With the rediscovery of the religious texts gShen chen klu dga was able to gather many disciples around him. Of these, three became very important for the subsequent four centuries of the development of *Bon*. One of them was Bru chen nam mkha gyung drung belonging to the family of *Bru*. His ancestors had migrated from *Bru sha* to Tibet. He founded the monastery of gYas ru dben sa kha to promote the study of the texts *mDzod phug* and *Gab pa*, two of his rediscoveries. The monastery of gYas ru dben sa kha became a great seat of learning for the *Bon po*. (It was destroyed in a flood in 1386. A.D.), A number of abbots of this monastery came from the *Bru* family, which was considered to be its patron. With the birth of two Panchen Lamas in this

16. Karmay, n.1, p.184.

family, its connexion with the monastery abruptly came to an end. The biographers of these two Panchen Lamas have taken great pains to avoid mentioning the religion of the family of *Bru*. Although they were lavish in their praise of the high nobility of the *Bru* clan in which the lamas were born, they deemed it unnecessary to mention the name of the religion of the family openly as it might undermine Their Holinesses in the eyes of the adherents of *dGe lugs pa*.[17]

Another prominent disciple was Zhu yas legs po. He belonged to the family of *Zhu*. Members of the *Zhu* family may still be found among the Tibetan refugees in India. Zhu yas legs po founded the monastery of sKyid mkhar ri zhing in the eleventh century A.D., which became an important centre of learning for those interested in rDzogs chen philosophy and practice.

The third important disciple was sPa ston dpal mchog. He belonged to the well-known family of *sPa*. He initiated the setting up of a hermitage which later developed into a centre of *tantric* learning.

Yet another disciple of gShen chen klu dga was rMe'u mkhas pa dpal chen. This disciple founded the monastery of Zang ri as a centre of philosophical studies.

Thus there were four *Bon po* centres in gTsang in Central Tibet. While two were concerned with scholasticism, the other two pursued spirituality and contemplation. In this period *Bon po* students roamed around not only visiting their own monasteries but also staying in those of the Buddhists such as *Sa skya sNar thang* and *gSang phu*. Buddhist scholars met *Bon po* monks in debate for philosophical disputation. For

17. Ibid., p.185.

example, it is said that Bu ston vanquished several *Bon po* in argument while he was studying.[18]

Sustenance for these large centres was provided by nomads living in the north. It came generally in the form of gifts consisting of animal produce. Most of the nomads of Tibet have been followers of *Bon* throughout Tibetan history. They supplied all the necessaries of life to the monasteries.[19] The *Bon po* at this time led a quiet religious life. They kept out of the religious and political squabbles of the Buddhist sects.

Towards the end of the fourteenth century, the various centres entered upon a period of decadence. However, with the arrival of the *Bon po* teacher mNyan med shes rab rgyal mtshan (1356-1415 A.D.), a new era began. He founded the monastery of sMan ri in 1405 A.D., which remained a most important *Bon po* centre till 1959. In 1834 A.D. another monastery was founded in gTsang by zLa ba rgyal mtshan (born in 1796 A.D.). It was called gYung drung gling. It had two hundred rooms and was one of the largest *Bon po* monasteries. Some time later yet another monastery called mKhar sna was established, near sMan ri. Thus there arose three important *Bon po* centres in Central Tibet.[20]

The quiet life lasted from 1017 AD to 1386 AD. It then came to an end with the coming to power of the theocratic government of the *dGe lugs pa.* The *Bon po* then once more suffered persecution along with the *Jo nang pa* sect, under Dalai Lama V. Several *Bon po* monasteries were turned into monasteries of the *dGe lugs pa.* In Kham the Buddhist ruler used his Mongol soldiers

18. Ibid.
19. Ibid.
20. Ibid.,p.186.

to subdue his religious opponents. However, the *Bon po* were spared the fate that befell the *Jo nang pa* who were totally banished from Tibet. This persecution continued for quite some time, in one place or another. rGya rong, a *Bon po* stronghold, successfully resisted Manchu encroachment for several years. The Emperor Qianlong, feeling helpless, asked his spiritual instructor lCang skya rol pai rdo rje (1717-86 A.D.), who is said to have been a *dGe lugs pa* incarnation, to use his magic powers against the uncompromising *Bon*. This spiritual instructor lost no time in taking this opportunity to vanquish the heretics by using the Chinese army. Although the Manchus failed to wean the people of rGya rong away from the *Bon* religion, they did manage to destroy the famous *Bon po* monastery of gYung drung lha sding and to erect in its place a *dGe lugs pa* monastery called dGa' ldan. The Emperor issued a proclamation prohibiting the practice of the *Bon* religion. And yet, in the face of such difficulties and discouragements, the *Bon po* stood loyal to their faith.[21]

In the later half of the nineteenth century there arose new developments especially in the philosophy of *rDzogs chen*. This was due to the *Bon po* teacher, Shar rdza bkra shis rgyal mtshan (1858-1935 A.D.), in Kham. He was one of those who initiated the *Ris med* movement (Universalism). In the light of his writings *Bon po* tradition developed in the same way as the *rNying ma pa* and in the same period, the impetus probably coming from the latter. The monastery of Khyung lung dngul mkhar was founded near Mount *Ti se* in 1936 by a lama, Ka rgya khyung sprul 'jigs med nam mkhai rdo rje (born 1897 AD.). By the beginning of the twentieth century there

21. Ibid.

were three hundred and thirty *Bon po* monasteries in Tibet.[22]

Our study leads to the following conclusions :

1. There are many difficulties in the way of giving a clear definition of the *Bon* religion. The term "*Bon po*" refers to an adherent of this faith. It also refers, in a narrower sense, to its class of exorcists and priests.

2. This religion has been characterized by a great regional diversity since the most ancient times. Each clan and locality has had its own *Bon* and transmitted it as such to the younger generations.

3. There can be no doubt about foreign influence on the *Bon* religion.

4. To start with, *Bon* was primarily concerned with rituals and magical practices directed at the overthrow of hostile powers or aimed at keeping them in check or at appeasing them. It was also concerned with ensuring that the dead did no harm to the living. Hence the elaborate ritual for the dead and their burial.

5. Doctrinal formulations represent a late phase in the development of *Bon*. They were specifically aimed at matching the rival religion, Buddhism.

6. In the *Bon* religion the concepts "sky" and "heaven" and the "god of heaven" play an important role. Equally important are the gods presiding over the soil and the earth, including the interior of the earth. Similarly the mountain gods and mountain ancestors are regarded as holy because of the belief that they descended from heaven over the mountains.

7. The summit of any of the sacred mountains was a place of contact between heaven and earth, the two

22. Ibid.

being linked by a sky ladder. Since this sky ladder was inadvertently cut, the two worlds of heaven and earth were severed for ever.

8. *Bon* divided the multitude of powers who inhabited this world into various groups according to their domain such as air, water, and the underground region. It later created its own iconography and assigned specific forms to those powers.

9. In course of time the distinction between *Bon* and Buddhism, especially in the *rDzogs chen* form, became thin. This occurred not only in the field of magical and exorcist practices, where the two religions often followed identical rituals for the good of an individual or of society, but also in the doctrinal field, though this represents a late phase of development. It would, therefore, appear that the two traditions, *Bon* and Buddhism, have existed side by side since the seventh century. The two have flowed together and given Tibet its unique religious culture.

CHAPTER FIVE

Bon's Encounter with Buddhism

Buddhism : Beginnings in India

Buddhism was born in India in the sixth century B.C.; it was introduced into Tibet in the seventh century A.D. During these thirteen centuries it underwent much change. Its founder, Siddhārtha, belonged to the ancient family of Gautama. The people hailed Him as the Buddha, "the Awakened One", in view of the enlightenment He had gained from the dream of life. The highlights of His life are well known and need not be recounted. An outline of His life story may, however, be in order here. He was born in the Śākya clan, which ruled a small principality at the foot of the Himālaya whose capital was Kapilavastu. At the age of twentynine, after spending an uneasy youth and becoming painfully conscious of the suffering which afflicted mankind as a whole, He renounced the world. He then embraced the life of a wanderer in quest of truth. As asceticism was the rule of serious life in that age Siddhārtha undertook severe penance, but this did not yield to Him what He was searching for. So He began a fresh course of self-discipline characterized by less rigour. In this second attempt truth at last flashed upon Him about the nature of suffering and the means of eradicating it. After a little initial hesitation He returned finally to the haunts of men and began the long and noble work of spreading among the people a knowledge of the truth that He had seen and which had brought Him freedom. He met with many difficulties as there were several doctrines contending for supremacy, but He persevered in His mission to relieve men and women of suffering. In the end He achieved extraordinary success. His teaching spread widely; eventually it grew into a world religion. He is one of the greatest figures in the spiritual history of mankind, and His life is one of the most inspiring in its lessons for humanity.[1] The Buddha lived for over eighty years. After spending four decades in spreading the truth He had discovered, he died near Kuśīnagara in the year 483 B.C. or thereabouts.

Teaching of the Buddha : *Hīnayāna*

The Buddha wrote no books. His teaching was put down in writing a long time after His death by his monk followers who had memorized His words and preserved them for their own benefit and for the enlightenment of mankind. Even early Buddhism was, therefore, characterized by elements which were the result of later thought and possibly also by elements older than the Buddha which, though not included by Him in His teaching, were afterwards incorporated by His followers responsible for assembling the canon.[2] The compilations, excluding the numerous commentaries, are known as Tripitaka, the Three Baskets of Tradition, or the threefold canon. They are : (1) *Suttas*, or utterances of the Buddha; (2) *Vinaya*, or rules of discipline; and (3) *Abhidhamma*, or philosophic discussions. Briefly, the teaching of the Buddha was in the form of a strictly philosophical theory of salvation for the elect. It was characterized by the

1. M.Hiriyanna, An Outline of Indian Philosophy (London, 1967), p.134.
2. Ibid., p.135.

Arhat ideal, the ideal of the religious individual who recognized, in the struggles of this world, the affliction of this life and overcame it by reaching a state in which the power of trsnā, or the life force, was broken, or in which all desire was effaced, and thus ultimately attained *nirvāṇa*.

It is true that the Buddha dwelt on the fact of evil, pain, or suffering, but He also pointed the way out of it. He did not recognize anything beyond the sphere of perception and reason. His teaching in its essence excluded whatever was not positively known. He taught only what was necessary for overcoming the evil which was the chief characteristic of life. Deliverance from pain and evil was His main concern. He was thus eminently practical.[3]

There is no metaphysics in the teaching of the Buddha.[4] In fact He was averse to mere theoretical curiosity. However, there is a good deal of philosophy underlying His teaching. Its main features are : (1) There is no self apart from the physical frame with which the self is associated. The word "self" is only a label for the aggregate of certain physical and psychical factors. In Sanskrit, it is known as *Nairātmyāvada,* or "the doctrine of no-self". According to this doctrine, both soul and matter exist only as complexes; neither of them is a single, self-contained entity. (2) Neither being nor non-being is the truth, but only becoming. There is incessant change, but there is nothing that changes : "There is action but no agent." It is a process, a process of coming to be and passing away. (3) There is an adequate reason for everything which explains why it is so and not otherwise. These reasons are completely, knowable. (4) Everything

---

3. Ibid., p.137.
4. Ibid., pp. 138-54.

changes from moment to moment. This is known in Sanskrit as *Kṣaṇikavāda* or "the doctrine of momentariness". Everything is in a state of flux; everything is being renewed all the time. (5) Each phase of experience, as it appears and disappears, is wrought up into the next. Every successive phase has within it "all the potentialities of its predecessors". These potentialities manifest themselves when conditions are favourable. (6) The material world is derived from five elements (*bhūtas*) on the physical side, viz. earth, water, fire, air, and ether (*ākāśa*). It is, therefore, termed *bhautika* to indicate its secondary character. On the psychical side, a rudimentary form, *citta*, is recognized; other features of the mind are termed *caitta* (derived from *citta*).

If all things in the world are transient and unsubstantial, our endeavour to secure any of them for ourselves or for others is vain. The very desire for them is delusion. More powerful than this desire for outside things is the craving for preservation of the self or the will to be. As there is no self, we should get rid of this craving to extinguish the pain of existence. Belief in the being of oneself presupposes belief in that of others and thereby gives rise to narrow love and hatred. With the elimination of the self, desire and suffering would disappear. As the belief in self-identity, which is the basis of suffering, is false, ignorance (*avidyā*) is the true source of all evil. This ignorance is of the four Noble Truths---those concerning suffering, its origin, its removal, and the way of removing it.

In the ultimate analysis the cause of suffering is ignorance and the evil it brings about. This is a process; its different stages represent a special causal formula known as the law of dependent origination or *pratīya-samutpāda*. It consists of twelve links (*nidāna*)---ignorance (*avidyā*), action (saṁskāra), consciousness (*vijñāna*), name and form (*nāma-rūpa*) the six fields (viz. the five senses and the mind together with their objects or *ṣaḍāyatana*), contact between the senses and the objects (*sparśa*), sensation (*vedanā*), desire (tṛṣṇā), clinging to existence (*upādāna*), being (*bhava*), rebirth (*jāṭi*), and pain or literally old age and death (*jarā-maraṇa*). It manifests the life that now is in its relation to the past as well as the future. It stands for a continually recurring series of births and deaths (*saṁsāra*). The first two links refer to the life immediately preceding the present one, meaning that it is the activity of the past life prompted by ignorance that gives rise to the present. The course of the latter is traced in the next eight links. The last two links refer prospectively to birth and suffering, which necessarily follow from the activities of the present life. Thus ignorance is the root cause of the individual's existence. From ignorance proceeds desire. Desire leads to activity. This in its turn results in rebirth with fresh desire. This is the vicious circle of never-ending births and deaths.

The removal of the cause must remove the effect. When ignorance is dispelled by right knowledge, the succeeding links of the chain snap one after another automatically.

The path of self-discipline which leads man to emancipation is eightfold - right faith, right resolve, right speech, right action, right living, right effort, right thought, and right concentration or meditation.

In His first sermon delivered in the deer park at Sārnāth near Vārāṇasi to His five former companions in the search for truth, the Buddha said that a person leading a truly religious life must aviod the two extremes, viz. a life of pleasure, or a life devoted to desire and enjoyment, which was base, ignoble, unspiritual, unworthy, and unreal, and a life of self- mortification, which was gloomy, unworthy, and unreal. The perfect individual is one who has discovered the way which lies between them. The Middle Path enlightens the mind and leads to peace, knowledge, and *nirvāṇa*.

Early Buddhism did not reject the gods and heaven of popular religion, but regarded them too as entities subject to the laws of development and decline in accordance with the law of *karma*. The Buddha recognized gods in the above sense, but He did not believe in God, the one immortal and immutable Supreme Being Who was above and beyond all laws. He held that the ego was only a conglomeration of life factors and that, with death, its bond was snapped. If salvation or *nirvāṇa* is not reached in this life, then it releases impulses which result in the origin of a new life. It is not the ego which is immortal, but only the sorrowful process of development and decline, and it is from this process that the Buddha sought to save mankind. It is thus a practical doctrine of salvation.[5]

Mahāyāna

The Buddha did not claim that He was the only enlightened one. According to Him, there had been Buddhas in the world from time immemorial. This led to speculation, and a mythology developed around six supposed predecessors of the Buddha viz. Vipaśyin, Śikhin, Viśvabhūti, Kakudsandha, Kanakamuni, and Kaśyapa. Further differences of opinion over the teaching and the regulations of the order led to the formation of a number of sects. This is clear from the reports of the different

5. Ibid.

Buddhist Councils. Up to the time of Aśoka the Great in the third century B.C., however, the Buddha's teaching appears to have retained its pristine purity. The famous edicts of that great ruler are evidence of this fact. Subsequently certain mythologies centred on Buddhist and popular divinities entered Buddhism, particularly of the lower orders such as the *Yakṣas* and the Nāgas.[6] By the beginning of the Christian era or thereabouts a new version of the Buddha's teaching was put out. Those who subscribed to this version called it *Mahāyāna*, or the Great Vehicle. Their ideal was *Bodhisattva* and universal salvation, as against the ideal of *Arhat* of the old order. They referred to the old order pejoratively as *Hīnayāna*, or the Small Vehicle. Whereas the *Arhat* strove only for personal salvation, the *Bodhisattva* was committed not to enter upon *nirvāṇa* until he had enabled every living thing to save itself.

With this Buddhism entered upon an emotional epoch. A large number of Buddha and *Bodhisattva* figures arose, who evoked devotion in the adherents of the religion. This devotion was not unlike the *bhakti* of the Hindus. In due course Buddhas like Vairocāna and Amitābha and *Bodhisattvas* like *Avalokiteśvara,* as also the Saviour of the coming world period, *Maitreya,* joined the Buddhist pantheon. Gradually some Hindu gods too entered Buddhism, including *Mahākāla-Śiva.* This was the time of the *Gandhara* school of art in northwest India. The artists belonging to this school of art came up with portraits representing the Buddha in stylized robes which remind one of the Greek manner. Then there was Nāgārjuna who perhaps lived in the second century A.D. and who is looked upon as the father of *Mahāyāna*

6. Helmut Hoffman, The Religions of Tibet, Edward Fitzgerald, trans.(London, 1961), edn 2, pp. 30-36.

Buddhism, with his *Mādhyamika* school. He taught that phenomenal existence and the life elements had no reality and that they were all empty (*sūnya*). He did separate *nirvāṇa* and *saṁsāra* materially but regarded them as more or less different aspects of an intangible and purely negative "emptiness" or "void".[7] Other *Mahāyāna* teachers like Asaṅga and Vasubandhu who were brothers, followed in the fourth or the fifth century. Asaṅga was the founder of the *Yogācāra* or *Vijñānavāda* school. Last in the series of *Mahāyāna* masters was Dharmakīrti in the seventh century A.D. and a contemporary of King Srong brtsan sgam po of Tibet.

Vajrayāna

The third stage in the development of Buddhism was *Vajrayāna*, or the Diamond Vehicle. Salvation was no more an arduous task as it had been thought to be in the time of the Buddha when sons of noble families abandoned their homes and devoted their whole lives to the search for truth. It was now held that salvation came in a flash, as it were, by the mere uttering of certain magic formulae. The onerous path of self-discipline and self- purification was for the spiritually untalented; the initiates took *Vajrayāna* or the direct path. For the sake of widening its appeal Buddhism now sought to assimilate more and more Hindu rituals. It included an increasing number of gods in its pantheon or created new ones. The texts of the Diamond Vehicle were not confined to a consideration of *siddhi,* or the highest perfection. They also dealt with such so-called magical processes as transmutation of base metal into gold, discovery of hidden treasures, changing one's shape or form, etc.

---

7. Ibid.

Simultaneously there were serious mystics who sought to unite with the absolute. This gave rise to the concept of Ādibuddha. Its highest peak of development is to be found in the *Kālcakra* system which was formulated in the light of the strong Hindu reaction to Buddhism and perhaps also under the influence of Western ideas.[8] It was in the time of Dharmakīrti that the erotic element entered *Vajrayāna*. Since then goddesses have been created and attached to particular Buddhas and *Bodhisattvas*. The polar antithesis of the world is supposed to find its resolution in the sacred and profane love of such divine pairs. The mystic copied such unification on earth according to a prescribed ritual with a consecrated woman known as *Śakti* or *Mudrā*. We may say that the history of the eroticized *Vajrayāna* begins with Saraha or Rāhulabhadra.[9] He came from a Brahmin family of Orissa but lost caste because he was used to the consumption of intoxicating liquor and lived with a low caste woman who served him as his *Mudrā*.

Form of Buddhism that Entered Tibet

Buddhism in all the forms outlined above came to Tibet in the seventh and eighth centuries A.D. Besides *Vajrayāna* which particularly occupied men's minds, the *Mahāyāna* of Nāgārjuna and Asaṅga and the *Hīnayāna* of *Sarvāstivādins* also entered Tibet. Together with Buddhism the art of writing too came since Srong brtsan sgam po, the then King of Tibet, realized that without a written language it was almost impossible to develop a higher culture and civilization. Indeed he sent one of his ministers, Thon mi sambhota, to Kashmir to learn the art of writing. This minister studied industriously under

8. Ibid.
9. Ibid

different masters and invented a script for the Tibetan language which met with its requirements. He also prepared textbooks of grammar. The new written language was used as a medium for the translation of Buddhist texts. The Tibetans, however, did not obtain their sacred texts and learned monks exclusively from India. They sought them out in China too, where Buddhism was already well established under the Tang dynasty.[10]

Srong brtsan sgam po

According to an old tradition, Tibet first established contact with Buddhism during the reign of King Lha tho tho ri, the fifth predecessor of King Srong brtsan sgam po. It is said that when King Lha tho tho ri was on the throne of Tibet, some books and a gold (or was it silver?) stūpa fell from the sky. Not able to decide what he should do with them, Tibet still being without a literary language, the King started worshipping them. The *Bon po* claimed that the books were *Bon* scriptures. What seems to have actually happened is that some Buddhist monks of Central Asia (or was it some Nepali monks?) came to Tibet with those scriptures to preach Buddhism and, finding that nobody understood their language, left them there and returned. According to this tradition, the introduction of Buddhism into Tibet dates back to the seventh century. (King Srong brtsan sgam po died in 650 A.D..) Not only was Tibet then unified, but it had emerged as a mighty Power, claiming suzerainty over a number of states in Central Asia. It was thus open to the cultural and religious influences of the highly civilized countries of China, India, and East Turkestan (which too had adopted Indian Buddhist culture). The King had a Nepali as well as a

10. Ibid.

Chinese wife. Both these women were Buddhists and had brought with them Buddhist images. The King erected Buddhist temples in Lhasa and other places for their sake. According to yet another tradition, the great *Bodhisattva Avalokiteśvara,* thinking the time ripe for converting the Land of Snow to the Doctrine of the Buddha, sent Srong brtsan sgam po as his own emanation and his Nepali and Chinese wives as emanations of *Tārā,* the divine consort of the *Bodhisattva.*[11]

It is possible that Buddhism was introduced into Tibet during the reign of Srong brtsan; for there are temples of that period like Jo khang (which has been greatly enlarged and transformed over the centuries), dBu ru ka tshal (east of Lhasa), Khra 'bong (in the Yar lung Valley), and Ra mo che (in Lhasa itself). There is no evidence, however, that the King himself adopted Buddhism. Nor is there any mention of Buddhism in contemporary literary sources. On the other hand the King seems to have been loyal to his ancestral religion, Bon. While choosing Buddhist symbols for the Ra mo che Temple, he consulted *Bon* priests as well. There was no conflict between Buddhism and the native religion of Tibet. Nor was there any imposition of a new or foreign religion. Srong brtsan was buried in the traditional way in the Yar lung Valley, where an enormous burial mound can still be seen.[12]

In introducing Buddhism into Tibet the King appears to have had political motives rather than religious. Through his conquest of a number of Central Asian states

11. Per Kvaerne, Tibet : The Rise and Fall of a Monastic Tradition, in Heinze Bechart and Richard Gombrich, eds, The World of Buddhism (London, 1984), pp.255-6

12. Ibid.,p.256.

and his contacts with India (including Kashmir), China, and Nepal, which were all flourishing centres of Buddhist culture, he became acquainted with certain elements of that culture, with its universalistic perspective, and felt that Tibet would do well to imbibe those elements without inviting any foreign political influence. Secondly, he wanted to introduce the art of writing into Tibet. He finally chose Buddhism from India and with it many other aspects of Indian culture, especially a literary language. One cannot, however, tell that Buddhism was really present in Tibet during the reign of Srong brtsan sgam po. It would appear that the King made use of the new religion for the advancement of culture. He did not establish any monastery; he only built a few temples. It is only in the following century, i.e. during the reign of King Khri srong lde brtsan (740-97 A.D.), that one finds mention of Buddhism in official documents. King Khri srong lde brtsan too was favourably inclined to Buddhism presumably from political considerations although later traditions hail him as the Second King of the Law and as an emanation of the *Bodhisattva Mañjuśrī*. In any case it is clear that Buddhism was established in Tibet under Royal patronage and that it served to increase Royal power. The native priests, who did not like the progress that the new religion was making in Tibet, made common cause with certain noble families against the King. After a bitter struggle, which seems to have taken the form of palace intrigue, the King and the Buddhist party gained the upper hand, and the task of providing the law, *Dharma*, on a firm basis began.[13]

---

13. Ibid.

Khri srong lde brtsan

During the reign of the two immediate successors of Srong brtsan sgam po, Buddhism made little progress. However, the political situation in the country was consolidated, and Tibet acquired a decisive voice in Asian politics. Khri srong was favourably inclined to Buddhism, but two of his ministers were much opposed to it. They managed to get even a ban imposed on it when he was a minor. Khri srong got rid of those ministers as soon as he came of age and invited the Indian scholar Śāntarakṣita to Tibet. He decided to set up a Buddhist monastery at bSam yas, southeast of Lhasa and on the northern bank of the gTsang po. This provoked opposition from the local priesthood and from some nobles, so much so that the King sent Śāntarakṣita back to India. After some time, seeing that the atmosphere was less hostile, he invited Śāntarakṣita again to Tibet, but Śāntarakṣita declined the offer. Instead he suggested the name of his brother- in-law, Guru Padmasambhava, who was a *tantric* master better equipped to tackle the situation which obtained in Tibet at that time. Padmasambhava was a native of Swat in the extreme northwest of India. He played a crucial role in the introduction of Buddhism into Tibet. While Śāntarakṣita was a representative of the conventional Vinaya-based monasticism and the *Sūtra*- inspired philosophical tradition of the *Mahāyāna*, Padmasambhava was a siddha, an adept at magical rites and a master of techniques of subduing demonic forces. The influence of Padmasambhava and that of the *Mahāyāna* philosophical tradition as taught by Śāntarakṣita have been predominant in Tibet ever since.[14]

14. 14.Ibid.

Padmasambhava

Guru Padmasambhava, known as "Lotus Born",[15] or "Rin po che", or "Precious Guru", or the "Second

---

15. For the legendary history of the birth of Guru Padmasambhava, see L.Austin Waddel, Buddhism of Tibet or Lamaism (Cambridge, 1959), pp.380-1. According to Waddel, the story itself is somewhat romantic. It has the widest currency in Tibet, where all the sites sacred to this deified wizard-priest are now popular places of pilgrimage. Waddel says that once upon a time, in the great city of Jatumati on the Indian subcontinent, there dwelt a blind King named Indrabodhi, who ruled over the country of Udyana or Urgyan. The death of his only son plunged the palace in deepest sorrow. This calamity was followed by famine and an exhausted treasury. In their distress the King and the people prayed to the Buddha with many offerings. Their appeal went up to the paradise of the Great Buddha of Boundless Light, Amitābha, who sent, as in a lightning flash, a miraculous incarnation of himself in the form of a red ray of light to the sacred lake of that country.
The same night the King dreamt a fair dream. He dreamt that a golden thunderbolt had come into his hands, and his body shone like the sun. In the morning the Royal priest, Trignadhara, reported that a glorious light of five rainbow- tints had settled in the lotus lake of Dhanakosha. It was so dazzling as to illuminate the three "unreal" worlds.
Then the King, whose sight was miraculously restored, visited the lake and, taking a boat, proceeded to see the shining wonder. He found, on the pure bosom of the lake a lotus-flower of matchless beauty, on whose petals sat a lovely, eitht- year-old boy, sceptred and shining like a god. The King fell on his knees and worshipped the divine child, exclaiming: "Incomparable boy, who are you? Who is your father, and which is your country?" The child replied, "My father I know. I come in accordance with the prophecy of the Great Ś'akyamuni, who had said,

Buddha"[16] in Tibet and in the adjacent Himalayan regions of India like Ladakh, Lahaul, Spiti, Kulu, and Manali, was a unique personality in the eighth century. Although he is not without critics, he is revered by all sects of Tibetan Buddhism. He occupies a place of prominence, sometimes along with the Buddha. An image of him is worshipped in all important monasteries of Tibet, particularly in the *dGe lugs pa* monasteries of Se ra, Dre spungs, and dGa' ldan. The historic fact that during the later part of the eighth century Padmasambhava was recommended to the King of Tibet by some of India's most famous scholars as one who was the greatest master of the occult sciences then known, testifies to the high esteem in which the Great Guru was held by his contemporaries.[17]

Around Padmasambhava are centred legends, mythologies, doctrinal systems, hierarchies of deities, and root teachings of Mahāyāna Buddhism embellished with all the glamour of Oriental imagery. His field of action was the cosmos; his religious mission embraced every sentient creature in all the worlds above and below. He

---

'Twelce hundred years after, in the northeast of the Urgyan country, in the pure lake of Kosha, a person more famed than myself will be born from a lotus and be known as Padmasambhava, or the Lotus-Born, and he shall be the teacher of my esoteric mantra-doctrine and shall deliver all beings from misery.'

One this the King and his subjects acknowledged the supernatural character of the boy. They conducted him to the palace with Royal honours. And from then onwards the country prospered, and the holy religion became vastly extended.

16. Waddel, n.15, p.33.
17. W.Y. Evans-Wentz, ed., *The Tibetan Book of the Great Liberation* (London, 1969), p.25.

was acclaimed master of all human arts and crafts and systems of philosophy, as an initiate of the occult sciences, as one perfect in yoga and transcendent over good and evil and immune to illness, old age and death and not subject to birth and thus greater than even Gautama Buddha : "He is the idealized exponent of the divine wisdom practically applied."[18]

Padmasambhava grew up in that centre of syncretism in northwest India which has always been the gateway for the entry of foreign people and foreign influences into this country. In fact, more than the political upheavals caused by the Greeks, the Kushans, and others, it was the constant influx of outside spiritual and religious ideals which turned Eastern Iran, Udyana (near Swat), Gandhara, Bru sha, Shang shung, and Kha che into a real cockpit of divergent religious beliefs---a circumstance which naturally had its effect on what was at that time the most influential and widespread Indian religion, viz. Buddhism. The major spiritual and religious influences operating in the eighth century in the days of Padmasambhava were Hellenism, the great scientific theories and the gnostic systems, the antique schools of mysticism, and Zoroastrianism in its orthodox and heretical forms besides Islam, the primitive beliefs of the West Himalayan districts and the *Bon* religion. Further, Manichaeanism, that world religion founded by the Babylonian Mani in the third century A.D., appears to have spread eastwards and influenced Buddhism, particularly its *Mahāyāna* and *Vajrayāna* forms.[19]

Legends attached to his birth and every action in life are varied. According to certain learned lamas, when

18. Ibid., p.31.
19. Hoffman, n.6, pp. 50-51.

the Buddha was dying, He had said: "I will take rebirth as Padmasambhava for the special purpose of preaching the esoteric Dharma." This belief appears to be based on a passage in the *bKa' gyur* which says that when the Buddha was about to pass away, He was asked why He had not taught the tantric mysteries. To this He is said to have replied : "Having been born out of a human womb, I am not fit to do so. I need to attain superhuman birth in order to enjoy the pure body through which alone the secret doctrine of the tantras can be revealed." He is then reported to have added : "In the worlds above I shall convoke a vast assembly of the Great Ones from the Ten Directions and a decision shall be made as to whether or not the tantric mysteries are at all to be taught." The Tibetan Buddhists, therefore, believe that after casting off His body, the Buddha convened a divine assembly in which a favourable decision was reached. Accordingly He once more took birth on earth as Padmasambhava. The tenth day of the fifth month of the Tibetan calendar is celebrated each year in commemoration of the incarnation of the Great Guru.[20]

Apart from these legends Padmasambhava appears to have been a native of Udyana in the northwest of India and to have been adopted as a son by King Indrabodhi of Urgyan near Bodh Gaya. The inhabitants of his native place were adherents of *Mahāyāna* Buddhism especially devoted to magic and exorcism. According to the biography written by his chief disciple, the Lady Ye shes 'tsho rgyal, Padmasambhava was ever active even as a child.[21] His early life as the prince and his renunciation resemble those of the Buddha. From his early childhood he was given to meditation. To distract him the King got

20. Evans-Wentz, n.17, p.28.
21. Ibid., p.104.

him married. And yet he renounced the world and became an ascetic to study the teaching of *Hīnayāna* and then the magic lessons of the *tantras*. He wandered restlessly throughout India and the adjacent Buddhist countries like many other Buddhist holy men. In the process he studied numerous sciences and particularly the secret teaching of a number of masters he came in contact with. He visited Śītalavana, where he devoted himself to necromancy and underwent several initiations by female spirits known as *Ḍākinīs*. He studied *Yoga* in India and also philosophy, logic, and the secret sciences. In the end he obtained the immortal *Vajra* body. In the kingdom of Zahore he performed miracles and won the heart of the daughter of the King of the country, Mandarva, and married her in secret. Mandarva accompanied him wherever he went. The King learnt of the marriage, had them captured, tied them to a stake, and set fire to them. But the fire turned miraculously into a lake, said to be the same as the Riwalsar Lake in Himachal Pradesh. (This lake is sacred to Buddhists and Hindus alike through its connextion with *Śiva* and *Pārvatī.*)[22]

In India Padmasambhava defeated those who taught heretical doctrines. He also worsted those who challenged him to magic contests. In Nepal he meditated in the rocky grotto of Yang le shod, a holy place which is still held in high honour. He even got the better of demonic forces when they tried to overthrow him. He thus won the highest perfection named *Mahāmudrā* or the Great Symbol.[23]

---

22. David L.Snellgrove, Buddhist Himalaya (Oxford, 1957), pp.150- 6. See also Hoffman,n.6, p.53.
23. Hoffman,n.6, p.55.

It was then that he received the invitation of the King of Tibet, Khri srong lde brtsan, to come and overthrow the demons of that land. These demons were opposing the introduction of Buddhism into Tibet. This King, being the son of a Chinese princess, had inherited through his mother a strong prejudice in favour of Buddhism. He succeeded to the throne when only thirteen years old. A few years later, seeing the general resistance to Buddhism, he decided to get a celebrated Buddhist priest from India to establish an order in Tibet. Śāntarakṣita advised him to secure, if possible, the services of his brother-in-law Guru Padmasambhava.

Padmasambhava accepted the invitation, went to Tibet in 747 A.D., and overthrew the demons one by one, obtaining an oath from them that thenceforth they would serve only the cause of the Buddha. He subdued them to his will and made them Protectors of Religion and admitted them into the enormously enlarged syncretive pantheon of Lamaism. The Tibetans who were steeped in superstition and felt themselves besieged on every side by malignant devils, welcomed the Guru in the fervent belief that he had brought them deliverance from their terrible tormentors. The Guru's most powerful weapon is said to have been the *Vajra*, symbolic of the Thunderbolt of Indra, and the spells extracted from the *Mahāyāna* Gospel. In 749 A.D., with the patronage of King Khri srong lde brtsan he established the first large monastery of Tibet at bSam yas, thirty miles from Lhasa, and fashioned the construction of this monastery after the model of Odantapuri of Magadha in East India. To this day it is one of the most important monasteries of Tibet.[24]

24. Waddel,n.15, pp.24 and 28.

Although Padmasambhava succeeded in breaking the resistance of the resentful and suspicious Tibetan nobles, yet their opposition did not die out. The nobles were particularly unreconciled to the fact that he had a number of wives, besides Mandarva. One of these wives had once been a wife of the King himself. They poisoned the ears of the King by carrying tales against his miracles. The King finally decided to send him back to India.[25]

Padmasambhava is considered to have been the founder of Lamaism.[26] "Lama" is a Tibetan word, meaning a man of superior status, and corresponds to the Sanskrit "*Uttara*". Its use was restricted to the head of a monastery. It is strictly applicable only to the abbots and the highest monks although, out of courtesy, the title is now given to almost all Tibetan Buddhist monks and priests.

It is not easy now to ascertain the exact details of the creed- primitive Lamaism-taught by the Guru; for all the works attributed to him were composed several centuries later by followers of his twentyfive Tibetan disciples. His name today is intimately associated with the essentials of sorcery and the special beliefs of the adherents of the old, unreformed sect, the *rNying ma pa*, who profess and are acknowledged to be his immediate followers and whose older scriptures date back to within two centuries of the Guru's time. It is evident that his teaching related to that extremely magical type of *Mahāyāna* Buddhism which then obtained in his native country Udyana and Kha che. And to this highly impure form of Buddhism, already overladen with much foreign accretion and saturated with demonolatry, was added a portion of the rituals of the indigenous *Bon po* religion.

25. Hoffman,n. 6, p.56.
26. Waddel,n.15, p.24.

Each of the demons accepted from the *Bon* religion was assigned a place of its own in the Lamaist pantheon.[27]

Thus the Guru gave a form to Buddhism which proved attractive to the people, and it soon became popular. Its doctrine of *karma*, or of ethical retribution, appealed to the fatalism which the Tibetans shared with most Eastern races. The priests of the native religion actively opposed the new religion, and they were supported by one of the most powerful ministers. Some of the so-called demons traditionally considered to have been overcome by the Guru were probably human adversaries. It is also stated that the *Bon po* were prohibited from making human and other bloody sacrifices according to their custom. Instead they were asked to adopt the practice of offering images of men and animals made of dough.[28]

Padmasambhava had twentyfive disciples. Each of these is credited with magical power and is of grotesque character. Padmasambhava instructed his disciples in making magic circles for coercing the demons or for exorcising them.[29]

The Guru made an attempt to found a religion of his own in Tibet. He succeeded to some extent as his doctrine was adopted by the *rNying ma pa* sect, which honours him to this day. This sect has held a specific and independent place of its own in Tibet, its internal squabbles and other trends notwithstanding. Padmasambhava could not carry out his mission in its entirety. This is clear from his premature departure from Tibet in the face of opposition from the *Bon* priests and politically powerful ministers.[30]

---

27. Ibid., 3pp.26-27.
28. Ibid., p.31.
29. Ibid., p.32.
30. Hoffman, n.6, p.58.

Evidence regarding the length of Padmasambhava's stay in Tibet differs. While the *rNying ma pa* regard the Guru's stay in Tibet as extending to the reign of King Khri srong's son and second successor Mu tig brtsan po and Sad na legs (798-817 A.D.), the historian Sum pa mkhan po, on the basis of archival records, declares that Padmasambhava spent just eighteeen months in Tibet. Some people go so far as to believe that the Guru stayed for fifty years. This does not seem to be credible. Howsoever long or short the period of his stay, there can be no doubt about the historical importance of the Guru. Padmasambhava had a very powerful influence on the development of Tibetan Buddhism. He founded a special religious tradition which has survived to the present day and, despite opposition from other sects, maintained its own special features.[31]

The most serious criticism directed against the Guru by those who disapprove of his *tantric* teaching is that he disregarded all commonly recognized standards of right and wrong, that he was a slave to strong drinks, and that he allowed the use of wine among his followers. To this charge his devotees' reply would be somewhat as follows: "Yes, it is true that the Precious Guru did drink to the point of intoxication and taught his disciples to do likewise. But the liquor is the ambrosia of the gods, the elixir of life, the nectar of immortality. They who quaff deeply of it become so intoxicated that they lose all consciousness of the world of appearances."[32]

In most images and paintings of Padmasambhava he is represented as holding, in his left hand, a human skull

---

31. Ibid.
32. Evans-Wentz,n.17, pp.31-32.

symbolic of the renunciation of saṁsāra. The skull, like a cup, holds divine liquor. Padmasambhava offers the drink to all those who choose him as their Guru and bids them drink of it and so attain liberation. In Sufism the drinking of wine and intoxication have the some esoteric significance. Among modern Hindu *tantrics,* those who are exotericists, drink wine, eat flesh, and provide for the union of *Śakti* and *Śākta*. But those who are fully initiated ensure that these things are done only symbolically. When Padmasambhava was accused of conjugal irregularties, he forgave his critics and thought to himself: "These fellows are ignorant of the inner significance of the *Mahāyāna* and of the Yogic practices appertaining to the three chief psychic nerves. I should pardon them."[33]

The Guru's mission was to overthrow unrighteousness and establish *Dharma*. It is, therefore, essential that he be judged, not from the viewpoint of his critics, but from his own viewpoint. According to his teaching, life is a fabric of correlative, interdependent, interacting dualities and cannot be understood without knowing both aspects of the dualities. Liberation comes upon the attainment of that state of transcendence in which all dualities fade away into undifferentiated wisdom. Failure to recognize the supreme law of the inseparableness of good and evil, of white and black, of positive and negative, constitutes ignorance or *avidyā*. This ignorance impedes self-realization; hence it is evil. It inhibits man from attaining full enlightenment or Buddhahood.[34]

Tantra teaches understanding and sublimation of the chief force in humanity, viz. the reproductive force. It is

33. Ibid.
34. Ibid., pp.37-54.

opposed to the more common and scientifically unsound teaching which advocates the forcible suppression of it. All the sciences and all the religions now recognize that there is a direct relationship between the highest psychic forces in mankind and the secretions of the sex glands so that physical youthfulness and efficiency depend upon conservation of the reproductive essences. Sex energy and spiritual growth are inseparable. Hence, without at least some general comprehension of Padmasambhava's *tantricism* one is likely to miss the point.[35]

Evans-Wentz in his assessment of the Guru quotes one of his own gurus as follows :

> It is unnecessary to give overmuch consideration to the opinions of the vulgar concerning the Precious Guru. The self-evident fact is that no one save a great master of Yoga could have written the "Yoga of Knowing the Mind in Its Nakedness", the authorship of which is accepted as being his. No man of uncontrolled appetites and passions could have conceived such a supreme teaching. When, too, there is taken into account the historic fact that Padmasambhava as the specially invited guest of King Khri srong lde brtsan was the first great teacher of the Doctrine of the Enlightened one to the people of Tibet, that he lifted them socially from crude barbarism to unsurpassed religious insight, that all sects of Tibetan Buddhists revere him, the Precious Guru cannot but be regarded as one of the Chief Cultural Heroes and Enlighteners of our common humanity.[36]

As to the criticism of the Guru's teaching on good and evil, or right and wrong, Evans-Wentz thus summarizes the essentials of the moral standard of Oriental sages, which alone should govern our judgement of the Guru:

---

35. Ibid., pp.62-63.
36. Ibid., p.35.

1. Good and evil, when viewed exoterically, are a duality, neither member of which is conceivable or capable of mentally existing independently of the other. Being thus inseparable, good and evil are intrinsically a unity.

2. A thing is considered either good or evil in accordance with the mental state in which it is viewed, this mental state itself being determined by the racial, social, or religious environment and heredity. Otherwise stated, as by Shakespeare, there is nothing good or bad, but thinking makes it so.

3. There being nothing which has other than an illusory existence in the mundance mind, nothing can be said to be either good or evil per se.

4. In as much as it is the motive and intent initiating an act which determines its character, no act, in itself, can be either good or evil; for the same act when performed independently by two persons, one with altruistic and the other with selfish motive and intent, becomes both good and evil.

5. There being nothing which is good per se or evil per se, good and evil, like all dualities, are hallucinatory concepts of the *saṁsārically* constituted mind of the percipient. As such, like the world of appearances, they have only a relative, not an absolute or true, existence.

6. Hence doctrines concerning a state of absolute evil called Hell and a state of absolute good called Heaven, are based entirely upon *saṁsārically* born concepts and are entirely relative and illusory. *Nirvāṇa* is beyond good and evil.

7. Accordingly all standards of morality founded upon any such doctrines are unstable; and, like saṁsāra itself, by which they are circumscribed, from which they arise, and upon which they are dependent for their illusoriness, they are ever-changing and transitory, like the mundane mind of their creators and advocates and, therefore, unsatisfactory and unfixable.

8. Not until mankind transcends dualism and phenomenal appearances and realizes the natural

at-one-ment of all living creatures, will they be able to formulate a sound standard of morality.

9.Such a standard will be based entirely, not partially, as are the prevailing standards of morality, upon world-wide *Bodhisattvic* altruism.

10. Its golden rule may be stated thus : Do unto others and to yourself only that which fosters Divine Wisdom and Will. Guide every sentient being to the Bodhi Path of transcendence over the *saṁsāra* and to the final goal of deliverance from ignorance.[37]

When Padmasambhava left, it was reportedly to the great sorrow of all; for a great multitude assembled to witness his departure. He summoned a chariot from the sky and, accompanied by two of his consorts, rode off to the south, to the "Yak-tail Continent" (India), to deal with the demons there. Many Tibetans believe that he is still alive using his powers for the good of the people.[38]

In any case Padmasambhava turned his visit to Tibet into a triumphant march: he carried everything before him. He is said to have subdued all inimical forces one after another. He spared their lives only when they swore a solemn oath, saying that they would help preserve the doctrine of the Buddha. This process is described colourfully in the form of a legend, perhaps to assimilate or accommodate the local deities of Buddhism. What happened in Tibet happened all over Asia. "Purged of elements, especially human and animal sacrifice, which are incompatible with basic Buddhist values", the local deities were assigned a secure, though modest, place in religious life.[39] They were generally regarded as beings "of this world". Their power was limited to granting

37. Ibid:, pp.56-57.
38. Thubten Jigme Norbu and Colin M. Turnbull, Tibet : Its History, Religion, and People (London, 1969). p.167.
39. Per Kvaerne,n.11, p.259.

worldly blessings unlike that of the great *Bodhisattvas* who could help their devotees towards liberation.

Padmasambhava completed the construction of the monastery at bSam yas. The monastery was consecrated in the presence of the King, possibly in the year 779 A.D., (This first monastery still stands though in a dilapidated condition.) Padmasambhava ordained seven Tibetans, traditionally referred to as the "seven elected ones", as Buddhist monks. (They became the first to accept Buddhist monkhood in Tibet). Buddhism was firmly established in the country though its influence was confined to court circles. According to an inscription preserved at bSam yas, King Khri srong and his ministers swore an oath to uphold the Buddhist Law. Monks belonging to noble clans were appointed ministers and given a higher rank than their lay colleagues. It is reported that at Royal receptions a monk was placed on the King's right side on the dais itself, while the ministers were seated below. Thus a notable characteristic of the Buddhist hierarchy in Tibet emerged from the very start, viz. its superiority over lay authorities.[40]

Conflict with *Bon*

Meanwhile the nobles who were opposed to Buddhism recognized that the *Bon* religion was no match for the spiritual and cultural powers of the "foreign" religion, the "interloper". To defeat Buddhism with its own weapons, therefore, they decided that the *Bon* religion should have a literature and a philosophic/religious doctrinal structure comparable to the Buddhist. To that end they invited *Bon* priests from Shang shung, a country which was independent at that time. (It is now a part of

40. Ibid.

Tibet. It lies west of Mount *Ti se.* It had its own language and its own political character; and on account of its situation was subject to a variety of influences such as Buddhism, Hinduism, and certain minor religious systems of West Asia.) Men from Shang shung were perhaps behind the mythical gShen rab, the founder of the *Bon* religion. Translations of the first Tibetan *Bon* texts were made from the language of Shang shung. This laid the basis of the future *Bon* canon. Besides, one of the wives of King Khri srong was a follower of the *Bon* religion. The King, though partial to Buddhism, was not sufficiently strong to have his own way altogether and was compelled to take the opposition of the Tibetan nobility and the *Bon po* into consideration. He counselled his followers to have patience, and observed that the *Bon* religion was strong among the people - far stronger than Buddhism.[41]

One day the King felt strong enough to follow his own dictates and to show clearly that he favoured Buddhism. A religious struggle followed, and possibly even a persecution of the *Bon po.* The *Bon po* were asked to accept the new religion. Those who did not were banished. The fleeing *Bon po* hid their books under rocks. (These were discovered later in the eleventh century A.D., They were called *gter ma*, or hidden treasures, and formed the nucleus of the *Bon bKa'gyur* and *bstan* 'gyur.) A large number of those who became converts to Buddhism did not forsake *Bon.* In fact, at heart they remained true to their religion. This was also the time when Tibetan monks visited famous Indian Buddhist universities like Nalanda and Vikramashilla. A number of Indian scholars were invited to Tibet to preach and propagate the Sacred Law.

41. Hoffman, n.6, pp.119-20.

Indian Buddhism versus Chinese Buddhism

A dispute arose between Indian Buddhist teaching and the Chinese reading of the Way of the Buddha. Matters of doctrine where the Chinese differed from their Indian counterparts related mainly to the following : (1) The Chinese insisted that the attainment of Buddhahood did not take place slowly as a result of protracted and tedious moral struggle for understanding, but suddenly and intuitively. This was in fact an idea taken from the Chinese Ch'an sect and the Japanese Zen sect. (2) Another point was the Chinese belief that meritorious actions of whatever kind, nay, spiritual striving itself, were evil. One must relieve one's mind of all deliberate thought and abandon oneself to complete inactivity. A debate was arranged at the court between Chinese and Indian scholars. It was a historic event from the viewpoint of the form of Buddhism that Tibet was to adopt and develop. Eventually the Indian side won, and consequently it was the Indian *Mahāyāna* version of Buddhism that was adopted in Tibet. This led to the expulsion of Chinese Buddhist teachers from the country.

Ral pa can

The struggle between the *Bon* religion and the Buddhist faith did not come to an end with the repressive measures of the King; for the *Bon po* enjoyed the support of powerful nobles. They remained more or less underground during the last years of the reign of Khri srong and his two successors (797-817 A.D). The next King, Ral pa can (817-836 A.D.), did his best to strengthen Buddhism in Tibet. He encouraged Buddhist literature, and a number of texts were translated. New translations were made only from the *Hīnayāna* and *Mahāyāna* originals from India. A list of books was drawn up which were deemed to contain the authentic teaching. The King's personal relations with the Buddhist monks were almost legendary. He left nothing undone to further the interests of the Buddhist clergy and to strengthen their position. Real power in the State passed increasingly into the hands of the Buddhists. Even the Prime Minister was a Buddhist. In the event of opposition the King invariably supported the Buddhists and punished those found guilty of any offence against Buddhism. The repression of all opposition to Buddhism led to conspiracies which isolated the King, and ultimately he was assassinated.

gLang dar ma and the Persecution of Buddhism

The victorious conspirators put a new king on the throne. He was King gLang dar ma (836-42 A.D). This King leaned heavily towards the nobles and the *Bon po*. All the important posts were awarded to the conspirators and their friends. Consequently a fierce campaign against Buddhism ensued. Everything possible to restore the *Bon* religion was done. Buddhist teaching was prohibited throughout the country. The work of translation of Buddhist texts was stopped. The temples of the Buddhists were closed down, their icons and idols removed and thrown out, and carefully translated texts destroyed by fire. The Buddhists tried to save a part of their literary treasures by hiding them in caves in the vicinity of Lhasa. The monks fled for their lives. Several were caught, tortured, and made to do humiliating tasks. Some others were killed while in fight. Those who remained behind were constrained to disown their religion and their priesthood. However, one day a fanatical Buddhist hermit, seeing the King reading an inscription on one of the many big obelisks set up earlier in Lhasa, shot an arrow and killed him. The murderer managed to escape by means of a disguise, leaving the capital and the whole country in utter confusion. Thus the reign of terror unleashed by gLang dar ma against the Buddhists came to an end.

Chaos and End of the Royal Dynasties

The consequences of these religious and political upheavals were negative for both *Bon* and Buddhism. The religious confusion and the struggle between the monarchy and the nobles weakened the once-so-powerful country to such an extent that it began to disintegrate. Before long it broke up into numerous small principalities. The authority of the Central Government was hardly operative outside the capital. Thus ended the rule of the dynasties. Both Buddhism and *Bon* suffered setbacks. For almost a century and a half darkness fell across Tibet. Hardly anything is known about this period. However, in the ensuing turmoil Buddhism as an organized religion disappeared - at least from Central Tibet. This is known as the failure of the first propagation of Buddhism. None the less a Tibetan literary language had been created, which remains more or less unchanged even today. Tibetan Buddhism became heir to the immense Buddhist literature of India (soon to be obliterated by Muslim invasions and the revival of the *Vedic* religion in its homeland). This literature enabled Tibetan monks to make their own contributions to Buddhist thought.[42]

42. Ibid.

CHAPTER SIX

Revival of Buddhism and the Rise of Different Schools of Buddhism

According to tradition, the upheavals that followed the rule of the dynasties did not lead to the complete disappearance of Buddhism from Tibet. Isolated Buddhist communities managed to survive in Central and West Tibet, as also in East Tibet along the Tibetan-Chinese boundary. Buddhist monks kept up their activity. There was thus no break in continuity. In West Tibet the descendants of the last dynasty had founded three kingdoms, viz. sMar yul, Gu ge, and sPu harangs. Buddhism in those kingdoms was strengthened by proximity to the Indian regions of Kha che, Bru sha, and Swat, which provided scholars, *yogis*, and artists. This facilitated the eventual restoration of Buddhism, which, according to tradition, was the "second propagation of the doctrine" in Tibet.

One of the principal initiators of this process of restoration of the Buddhist religion was Ye shes od, King of sPu harangs. He went so far as to abdicate in favour of his brother Srong nge to become a monk and took the religious name of lHa bla ma Ye shes od. His two sons also became monks. However, he did not renounce power altogether : he remained the head of State as priest-king.

His brother Srong nge looked after the business of Government from day to day as Viceroy. Ye shes od believed that the philosophy of *Mahāyāna* was based on the actual words of the Buddha. He doubted the validity of the claim that the *tantras* were based on the authentic pronouncements of the Enlightened One. He was extremely concerned about the moral laxity that Buddhist monks had permitted themselves and the aberrant practices that they had adopted in the light of their literal interpretation of certain *tantras*. He attacked those who offered bloody sacrifices and all kinds of impure substances to the deities, indulged in sex, and even performed weird rites to kill others and still claimed to follow *Mahāyāna*. Many Buddhist *tantric* adepts, not being steeled in monastic discipline and lacking in scholarly training, competed with the pre-Buddhist priesthood in acquiring and using magical power.

Ye shes od set to work to restore monastic discipline. He sent a group of twentyone young men to India, especially to Kha che, for training. Chief among the young men sent by him was Rin chen bzang po (958-1055 A.D). Not only was Kha che near but it was, together with Magadha in the east, an important centre of Buddhist studies at the time. It was in Kha che that most teachers and mystics of the various schools originated. Rin chen bzang po spent seventeen years in Kha che and elsewhere in India and became thoroughly familiar with *Mahāyāna* monasticism. On his return to Tibet he operated at two levels: He set up numerous chapels (*lHa khang*) in the territories under the King of Gu ge and its neighbouring regions and also undertook an intensive programme of

---

1. Per Kvaerne, "Tibet : The Rise and Fall of a Monastic Tradition", in Heinze Bechart and richard Gombrich, eds, The World of Buddhism (London, 1984), p. 259.

translation work and renewal of monastic discipline. Along with his collaborators he translated and revised as many as 158 Indian texts, both long and short. These were later included in the *bKa' 'gyur* and the *bStan 'gyur*. He is also credited with the establishment of important monasteries like Tabo in Spiti, sTod gling in Gu ge, and Nyar ma in Ladakh.[2]

All this religious activity met with much opposition from the *Bon po* in Shang shung, the centre of the systematized *Bon* religion. *Bon* was still powerful in this area at the time of Rin chen bzang po. As the building of numerous temples is supposed to have angered the local spirits, i.e. the *Bon* priests, Ye shes od deemed it expedient to subdue them. He reportedly refuted and defeated a good many followers of heterodox magical practices. A school formed itself around him with numerous disciples. Buddhism thus expanded through West Tibet and breached the solidarity of the *Bon* community.

This religious momentum spread to Central Tibet also. There was a continous stream of Tibetan pilgrims flowing into India. Such pilgrims included especially translators (*lo tsa ba*). They visited the sacred places of Buddhist tradition in India to collect books, to study in the different schools set up by well- known teachers and to secure initiation into *tantric* liturgy, and to receive instruction in the oral traditions of the mystic, ascetic, or *yogic* and *tantric* texts and practices. Indian teachers too crossed the Himalaya into Tibet quite often. They also went to Nepal in view of the revival of Hinduism in India and the increasing invasions of Muslim rulers from beyond the Khyber Pass. They carried with them their books and their protective dieties.[3]

---

2. Ibid.
3. Helmut Hoffman, The Religions of Tibet, Edward Fitzgerald, trans, (London, 1961), pp. 119-20.

Atiśa in Tibet

The Indian monk Atiśa (982-1054 A.D.), a native of Bengal and famous scholar-monk of Vikramashila University, provided much of the stimulus needed for the revival of Buddhism in Tibet during this period. He came in 1042 in response to a repeated invitation from a nephew of ye shes od's. This event owes much to the religious zeal and self-sacrifice of Ye shes od. Having heard of Atiśa as one of the leading scholars and mystics of the Buddhist faith, Ye shes od decided to invite him to Tibet and deputed a messenger for the purpose. He also presented a bar of gold to Atiśa to persuade him to come. This, however, failed to move Atiśa. Nothing daunted, Ye shes od sent the messenger again to Vikramashila to act as an observer and to look out for an opportunity to persuade Atiśa to visit Tibet. In spite of his religious vows, he also organized, as the commander of the army of Gu ge, a number of expeditions into neighbouring kingdoms and collected a large amount of gold in order to be able to invite Atiśa and other Indian scholars to his country. He also invaded the land of Gar log, but there he was defeated and taken prisoner. The captor said that he was prepared to release him and even to allow him to return to his own country if he became a vassal and adopted the religion of Islam. Or else he should pay his own ransom equivalent to his weight in gold. At this misfortune the followers of ye shes od and of the new Viceroy, Byang chub od, who was the son of Srong nge and a religious enthusiast, were plunged in deep sorrow. Byang chub od felt that to try to secure the release of Ye shes od by armed force was hazardous as the captors might kill him. He, therefore, collected a large amount of gold from people throughout Tibet so that he might ransom Ye shes od. When he had collected what he considered to be enough, he went with an escort to the court of the King of Gar log. There he discovered that the gold carried by him was enough only to ransom the body (i.e. trunk) of Ye shes od but not his head as well. He was, however, allowed to meet his uncle for a short interview. The prince found him sick and depressed. He also found that he had been kept in a dungeon for a long time. He did his best to console him and raise his spirits by telling him that he would collect more gold and return soon. Ye shes od replied that he was now an old man, broken by illness. His life was no longer of any value. Byang chub od should, therefore, use the gold he had collected to invite Indian scholars to the country. Ye shes od added that he would willingly sacrifice his life for the sake of religion. He said he was glad that his sufferings and death would be of some use to Buddhism. The two then parted with a heavy heart. Byang chub od returned to his own country to fulfil the King's wishes and invite Atīśa. This time Atīśa agreed to visit Tibet. As for Ye shes od, his captors murdered him in prision.[4]

Having arrived in Tibet, Atīśa set about purifying the then degenerate form of Tibetan Buddhism. He did not seek to abolish the study of the *tantras*, but endeavoured to harmonize the requirements of religious discipline, philosophy, and mysticism as well as he might. He insisted on monastic discipline and at the same time found room for the study and practice of the *tantras* in the monasteries. He stressed the importance of practising the conventional Buddhist virtues and of treading the long, strenuous path of a *Bodhisattva*. Many came to study under him, including the Royal monk Byang chub od (who had abdicated in favour of his brother 'Od lde).

4. Ibid.

Atīśa devoted himself to translation work. He also undertook some literary work. The most important fruit of his labours was *Bodhipatha-pradīpa* or the Lamp for the Way of Enlightenment, which represents the purest spirit of an elevated *Mahāyāna* aspirant such as had animated the best teachers of the Buddhist world. At the invitation of some of his followers Atīśa visited Central Tibet to further the cause of Buddhism there. Thereafter, he visited all the important sacred places and monasteries of Tibet and gathered pupils around him wherever he went. After staying in Tibet for thirteen years he died at the age of seventythree in sNye thang, south of Lhasa. He bequeathed his mantle to his disciple Brom.

Tantra

Simultaneously an entirely different kind of Buddhist practice was introduced into Tibet from Bihar and Bengal in India. This was the *tantric* kind, which stressed certain meditative procedures in line with the doctrines of Na ro pa, an Indian *siddha*. It was Mar pa (1012-96 A.D.), who pioneered it in Tibet. After studying for sixteen years in Bihar and learning Sanskrit thoroughly, Mar pa became famous as a translator of Buddhist texts and an accomplished *tantric*. His most famous disciple was Mi la re pa (1052-1135 A.D.), the cotton-clad ascetic who spent many years meditating in solitude in the higher reaches of the Himalaya and practising the various *yogic* exercises taught to him by Mar pa. It is said that among other things he developed the power to withstand the bitter cold of the Himalaya, clad only in a thin robe of white cotton. Mar pa and Mi la re pa represented a type of Buddhist *tantric* practice different from the monastic type that Atīśa represented. In fact neither of them was ever ordained a monk. The two are important in Tibetan

Buddhist literature inasmuch as they introduced a new kind of highly personal religious poetry which combined certain elements of the Indian *dohā* tradition with spontaneous feeling and observation.

Kālacakra

Atīśa is credited with a significant achievement, viz. a system of chronology of his own. He was in fact an adept at it, having been initiated into the subject by his teacher Na ro pa. The actual introduction of his system of chronology is connected with the adoption of the *Kālacakra* system in a systematized and simplified form. The history of the *Kālacakra* system is largely obscure, but there is no doubt that *Kālacakra* has played a great role in the history of Tibet (particularly in the history of the *dGe lugs pa*). It retains its importance even today.

"*Kālacakra*" means the Wheel of Time. Originally it referred to the animal cycle of twelve (hare, dragon, snake, horse, sheep, monkey, hen, dog, pig, mouse, ox, and tiger) used for reckoning dates not only in Tibet but throughout Central Asia. Later, by addition of a further cycle of constituents made up of a combination of the five elements (viz. fire, earth, iron, water, and wood), a cycle of sixty years was introduced to allow for a more accurate time computation. Astronomy and astrology are the basis of the whole system. The system in fact deifies the elements of astrology and raises them to the status of a means of salvation. At its back lies the ancient belief in the identity of microcosm and macrocosm. The most condensed expression of the belief is to be found in a magical device based on the dictum that the powerful one has ten forms (*daśākāro vaśī*), which can be seen

5. Per Kvaerne, n. 1,p. 260.

everywhere in Tibet. The symbolism embraces simultaneously all the power of the world and of the human body and the human spirit.

There are a number of legends regarding the origin of the system of *Kālacakra*. According to the basic tantra texts, the Buddha himself preached the *Kālacakra* teaching from the famous Vulture Peak near Rājagṛāha after his proclamation of *Mahāyāna,* the method of transcendental wisdom (*Prajñāparamitā*), and again at Dhanayakataka in South India, not far from the famous sacred mountain Śriparvata, which is closely associated with the legendary Nāgārjuna. Dhanayakataka must have been an important centre of Buddhist *tantric* practices. It is said that the Buddha himself, in his eightieth year, preached the esoteric teaching in the presence of numerous *Bodhisattvas* and deities and that King Sucandra of Shambala was also present at the time by some mysterious means. According to other sources, the system came from Shambala, a country of unknown description situated outside India somewhere in North Tibet or Central Asia - which has so far not been identified. It is believed that Shambala was surrounded by snow-capped mountains. In the centre of the country lay a magnificent city where the King had his palace Kalapa. To the south was a big park in which there was a *maṇḍala* of the *Kālacakra* built by King Sucandra. There was also a smaller *maṇḍala* built by one of his successors, Puṇḍarīka. It is further believed that the system was introduced into India sixty years before its introduction into Tibet. As the year 1026 A.D., is accepted as the time of its official introduction into Tibet, it follows that it came into India in 966 A.D., As for the master who was responsible for the introduction of

6. Hoffman, n 3,pp. 124-8.

the system of *Kālacakra* into India, nothing definite is known. Suffice it to say that a young monk named Tsi lu pa arrived in India with the system from Shambala in 966 A.D., He first went to East India and then travelled to South India where a minister, a Brahmin by caste, became his pupil. The young monk then went to Nalanda, which was a most important centre of Buddhism in those days, and reportedly wrote the microcosm-macrocosm symbol of *Kālacakra* over the gate of the monastery. The great scholar Nadapada, called Na ro pa in Tibetan, was the abbot of the monastery. He entered into a disputation with Tsi lu pa, was defeated, and became his pupil. In fact he became a prominent interpreter of *Kālacakra* and the teaching associated with it. The whole tradition of *Kālacakra* is derived from these two, not only in India but also in Tibet, where its introduction came sixty years later through their pupils. Even today it represents one of the fundamentals of the dominant *dGe lugs pa* sect in Tibet.[7]

As stated already, "*Kālacakra*" means the Wheel of Time. According to Buddhist tradition, there are two *Mahāyāna* paths leading to full enlightenment - personal liberation from suffering and the ability to liberate all others from suffering - the path of the *sūtras* and that of the *tantras*. Whatever the path chosen, the goal is the same - Buddhahood. The *tantras*, however, teach a more varied and a quicker means of attaining the goal. They have four different levels to suit the needs of different people. The most advanced level is the *anuttara yoga* which helps attain enlightenment in a few years of extremely intense meditational practice. This is itself divided into the father and mother classes, the father class

7. Ibid.

specializing in method and the mother class in wisdom. The *Kālacakra tantra* belongs to the mother class.

It is said that the teaching connected with the *Kālacakra* system has come down in a direct, unbroken line to His Holiness Dalai Lama XIV through his senior tutor, sKyab rje yong dzin ling rin po che, the nineteenth successor of Tsong kha pa. It was Cho kyi pal wa, disciple of Bu ston, the most experienced commentator on the *Kālacakra* system, who passed it on to Tsong kha pa. Tsong kha pa, after receiving this teaching, did a full meditational retreat on its six-facultied completion stage. At the successful conclusion of this retreat he had a vision of the *Kālacakra* deity. The vision, placing its hand on his head, prophesied that he would be like another King zLa ba bzang po for the propagation of the teaching. (The King was Sucandara of Shambala, who had received the teaching directly from the Buddha in South India.) It is significant that this *Kālacakra* line remains unbroken to the present day, for it is impossible to develop insights into a meditational practice if the line is disrupted.

There are three essential conditions which one must fulfil to qualify to take this speedier path. One must (1) renounce one's own unhappiness and unsatisfactory way of life; (2) develop the pure *Bodhicitta* motivation in order to become a Buddha and to liberate all others from their unhappiness; and (3) eliminate one's own ignorance by realizing *śūnyatā* or voidness which is the true nature of all things. These conditions are not peculiar to the *tantric* way of attaining elightenment but are equally applicable to other means available under *Mahāyāna*. Without being firmly based in the ground of renunciation and without developing the *Bodhicitta* motivation and without acquiring a right understanding of śūnyatā, one cannot attain solid and concrete experience from *tantric* practices. It is, therefore, important to have at least an intelligent understanding of these three subjects gained from hearing correct explanations before thinking about them and meditating on them.[8]

Kālacakra is perceived at three levels, viz. external, internal, and the alternative or opposite Wheel of Time. The external teaching concerns astronomy, astrology, and mathematics and represents the macrocosm which is the basis of phenomenal existence; the internal teaching concerns the microcosm, i.e. the structure of the human body, including its energy systems, and the alternative or opposite Wheel of Time is the study and practice of the actual *Kālacakra* meditational deity and his circular abode, the *maṇḍala*. The alternative or opposite Wheel of Time is the countervailing force against the deluding impact of the Wheel of Time and reveals the most fascinating doctrine of *Kālacakra* as also the methods of practice. With the exception of certain distinct aspects, the practice is akin to the sixfold esoteric practice of Na ro pa.[9] Full initiation empowers one to study and practise at all three levels in their proper, progressive order.

It is said that twentyfive propagators will rule throughout the universe some time in the future and spread a knowledge of *Kālacakra* once more. All those who have received initiation will be reborn fully ripe to attain enlightenment through this meditational practice. We are now in the reign of the twentyfirst propagator of *Kālacakra* - Dalai Lama XIV.[10]

---

8. Ngawang Dhargyey, "An Introduction to and an Outline of the Kalackakra Initiation", Tibet Journal (Dharamsala), vol,1, no.1. July-September 1985, pp.72-77. See also Ernst Haas and Minke Gisela, "The Kalachakra Initiation", Ibid, vol.1, nos 3-4, autumn 1976, pp.29-31.
9. Ibid.
10. Ibid.

Buddhist Schools

Different schools of Buddhism came into existence in the eleventh and twelfth centuries. All schools trace their origins to India, although they stress different aspects of Buddhism. They developed their own hierarchies and set about founding monasteries throughout Tibet. They also competed for the support of the laity and often engaged in bitter struggle for temporal power.

bKa' gdams pa School

The first school to come into existence was bKa' gdams pa. The name means "Bound by Command". This school insisted on the strict observance of monastic rules and, in particular, on abstention from marriage and travel, consumption of intoxicants, and possession of money. It was founded by Brom ston, chief disciple of Atīśa. Brom ston also founded the monastery of Rva sgrengs north of Lhasa in 1056 A.D. Adherents of the bKa' gdams pa school led a life of seclusion in study and meditation. It was a small school to start with and had no wealthy lay patrons. It, however, played a crucial role in later developments, i.e. in the developments which occurred in the later fourteenth and early fifteenth centuries, and was transformed in consequence into the *dGe lugs pa* school, which eventually attained both religious and temporal dominance in Tibet. It did not reject the *tantric* exercises of *Vajrayāna*, but it made a few modifications. It developed the exercises intelligently so as to steer clear of the aberrations and heresies into which the followers of Tibetan Buddhism had fallen in those days. Indeed it exerted a significant influence upon the development of Buddhist *tantric* practices in Tibet. Its masters enjoyed great prestige, so much so that the adherents of the other sects too came to study under them.

bKa' rgyud pa and Karma pa

Another important school was bKa rgyud pa. The name means "Follower of Transmitted Command". This school had a number of illustrious scholars and teachers going back in an unbroken spiritual line to Ti lo pa, Mar pa and Na ro pa. Ti lo pa is believed to have been a pupil of no less a teacher than the Buddha Vajradhara. bKa' rgyud pa represents a group of related schools such as the Karma pa and 'Brug pa schools. The name of sGam po pa (1079-1153 A.D.), the "Doctor from Dvag po", occurs in Tibetan Buddhist literature as one who received monastic ordination as a follower of the bKa' gdams pa school but who subsequently became a disciple of Mi la re pa. sGam po pa's direct disciples founded several famous schools, but there was little difference between those schools in matters of doctrine. The Karma pa school, founded by Dus gsuṁ mkhyen pa (1110-93 A.D.), a disciple of sGam po pa, had its principal monastery at mTshur pa in Central Tibet, which was founded in 1185 A.D. It was supported by the people in the neighbourhood of its monasteries, not by the members of any powerful family. The hierarchs travelled widely, surrounded by armed followers, the "men of the camp". In fact they had at their command a considerable military force and played an important part in the struggle for power in later centuries.

'Brug pa School

Then there was the school known as *'Brug pa.* The spiritual founder of this school was gLing chen ras pa (1128-88 A.D.), who founded (1180 A.D.), the monastery of Rva lungs southeast of rGyan tse, not far from the Tibetan-Bhutanese boundary. This school received its name from the monastery of *Brug* just north of the gTsang po. "Brug" means a dragon. The monastery is called *Brug* because a dragon is supposed to have appeared in the sky during its consecration. In the seventeeth century a branch of the '*Brug pa* school established itself in Bhutan, where it has remained dominant ever since.

The disciples of Mar pa can be divided into three groups : (1) those entrusted with the interpretation of texts (*bshad bka' dzin*); (2) the ascetics (*grub bka' dzin*); and (3) those whose task was to transmit esoteric practices through transfer of their consciousness into other beings, particularly into dead bodies. Mar pa's son Dar ma mdo sde received from his father this sacred teaching about the transfer of consciousness from one being to another, but he kept it to himself, and it was lost at his death. Mar pa's most important disciple was Mi la re pa (1040-1123 A.D). Mar pa initiated Mi la re pa into his mystical exercises. Mi la re pa was a poet. He composed numerous *dohās*, spelling out the doctrines of the school and the techniques of conducting mystical exercises. The *dohās* are written in a kind of allusive language which is often difficult to understand.

Phag ma gru pa (1110-70 A.D.), another disciple of sGam po pa, founded the monastery of gDan sa mthil, which rapidly grew large and wealthy, with the simple grass hut of the founder preserved in the centre. Its growth was made possible by the patronage of the noble family of Rva lungs. In course of time it became customary for this family to provide both the abbot and the lay administrative head of the monastery. While the abbot remained celibate, his lay counterpart continued the family line, so that the next abbot might be chosen from among

11. Giuseppe Tucci, Religions of Tibet (New Delhi, 1980), p.36.

his sons. The succession of abbots was thus provided for in a continual sequence of uncle and nephew, a pattern that was also followed in other schools. This union of spiritual and temporal power was an extremely significant development and explains the political preoccupations of many large Tibetan monasteries in the following centuries, as well as the armed conflicts that took place between them.

Sa skya pa School

Yet another school worth mentioning is the *Sa skya pa*, named after the monastery at *Sa skya*, west of Shigatse, in the province of gTsang. The founder of the sect was 'Brog mi (992-1072 A.D). 'Brog mi spent many years in India, studying under different masters, in particular Shanti pa, a *siddha*. He was initiated into a series of *tantras*, the most important being *Hevajra tantra*, and he translated the books relating to them into Tibetan. His disciple, dKon mchog rgyal po, founded the *Sa skya* monastery in 1073 A.D. He belonged to the powerful Khon family. The succession of abbots at *Sa skya* has been confined to this family and has taken the familiar uncle-and-nephew pattern. Being situated on the trade route between the Nepal Valley and Shigatse, *Sa skya* soon became a large and flourishing institution, with numerous affiliated monasteries famous for the learning of its teachers who were particularly active as translators of Indian texts. The power of this sect reached its apex in the thirteenth century. In 1244 Kodan, a Mongol Khan, summoned the head lama of *Sa skya* to his court and demanded and received from him the submission of Tibet. In return he appointed the *Sa skya* lama as his regent in Tibet. The

12. Per Kverne, n.1, p.261.

next head of the *Sa skya* monastery, Phags pa (1235-80 A.D.), succeeded in winning the confidence of Kublai Khan after participating in a magic display and establishing his superiority over Taoist and Nestorian Christian priests. Kublai Khan soon became Emperor of China and emerged as a powerful patron of Buddhism. Not only did he grant freedom from taxation to the monasteries in Tibet, but he also enabled the country to usher in an era of peace under a single political leadership. This leadership was that of a religious hierarchy. This is considered to be the origin of theocratic rule in Tibet. However, the power of the *Sa skya pa* declined with the Mongol dynasty in China. The coming of the Ming dynasty to power heralded the end of Tibetan dominance and the beginning of a period of struggle for power between the various Buddhist schools in Tibet, each school receiving support from its lay patrons.[13]

rNying ma pa School

One common feature of the schools described above is that they all originated in the eleventh century. There is, however, a school with a different background, viz. the *rNying ma pa* school. The name *rNying ma pa* means "Adherents of Old". This school traces its history to Padmasambhava or to the first propagation of the doctrine. i.e. to the eighth century. Its background was partly that of village *tantrics* whom King Ye shes od had criticized so severely, and partly that of a school of meditation known as the Great Perfection, which traced its practices back to Vairocana, a Tibetan disciple of Padmasambhava, and to other early figures. This school somehow managed to survive in East Tibet in spite of the decline of Royal

13. Ibid.,p.262.

power in Central Tibet. To those of the rNying ma pa school Padmasambhava was a divine figure, a second Buddha. The school had neither a central leadership nor an orgainized hierarchy. It avoided involvement in the political struggles of the times, and its monastic centres remained small and scattered. In the subsequent centuries it established conventional centres of monastic life on the model of those of the other schools. It also provided for the village *tantric* type of religious practitioners who often lived as householders and formed a distinctive social group or class and who only met in a local temple for the performance of rituals.

The *rNying ma pa* school accepted as authoritative a number of *tantras* supposedly introduced into Tibet at the time of Padmasambhava. Hence its name *rNying ma pa* or the Old Order. The other schools had rejected those *tantras* en bloc and had based themselves on other, new *tantras*. The adherents of the *rNying ma pa* school believed that Padmasambhava and his disciples had foreseen the troubles that lay ahead of Tibet and had hidden away a large number of texts in caves and in pillars, statues, etc. or had them buried in the ground so that they might be taken out and propagated later, when the time was propitious. Most texts were rediscovered as they had planned. They were called Rediscovered Treasures (*gter ma*). They hailed the lamas who rediscovered them as Revealers of Treasures (*gter ston*). The rediscovered texts included treatises on *tantras*, medicinal and ritual texts, manuals of meditation of the Great Perfection type, and a detailed biography of Padmasambhava. The critics of *rNying ma pa* rejected this literature, saying that they were spurious or fabricated. Recent researches, however, show that it does contain a good deal of ancient material. !14 This literature also reflects the national sentiment of the *rNying ma pa* scholars, and their glorification of ancient royalty was a kind of reaction to Mongol overlordship. Later efforts of the adherents of the *rNying ma pa* school were directed inter alia, at systematization of their literature. The great kLong chen lama (1308-64 A.D.), composed what were called Seven Treasuries in which he provided a detailed philosophical basis for the Great Perfection.

Meanwhile the other schools kept in constant contact with Buddhist centres in Nepal and India (Bengal, Bihar, and Kha che). The Tibetans were constantly going to India in search of texts, relics, and spiritual instructions. Indian saints and scholars also travelled to Tibet till the Muslim invasions of Bengal and Bihar towards the end of the twelfth century and of Kha che about a century later. This meant the complete disappearance of Buddhism from the land of its origin. Gradually the Tibetans started regarding their own country as the centre of the Buddhist world. It was in this period that belief in *Avalokiteśvara* as the patron deity of Tibet first gained wide acceptance.

We may here note in passing a significant development of this period which presents a characteristic aspect of Tibetan Buddhism, viz. the institution of succession by reincarnation. This term covers two somewhat different ideas. The Divine Kings were regarded as reincarnations of the different *Bodhisattvas*. On the same pattern every *Sa skya pa* lama was regarded as the reincarnation of some holy person or other. Soon this idea spread to other schools. There was a general tendency to regard one's spiritual preceptor as the visible

14. Ibid.,p.263.

15. Ibid.,p.263

manifestation of the Buddha. However, within the Karma pa school the successor of a deceased head lama was sought in a child who, by certain signs indicated that he was indeed the reincarnation of the former. A noteworthy fact is that this idea developed within a school where there was no dominant family line.[16]

The work of translating Indian Buddhist texts, which had been going on for centuries, came to an end by the fourteenth century. The editing of this enormous mass of translations yielded a canonical work known as *bKa' gyur*, a word which means "Word of the Buddha". The canon consists of 108 volumes. It is associated with the name of the great scholar Bu ston (1290-1364 A.D). It contains the *Vinaya* texts, the *Mahāyāna sūtras*, and the *tantras*, Bu ston also undertook a similar compilation known as *bStan' gyur*. This compilation consists of 225 volumes and contains commentaries and treatises. The *bKa' gyur* and the *bStan' gyur* were later translated into Mongolian. In the course of the fourteenth century the adherents of the *rNying ma pa* school compiled a voluminous compendium of the old *tantras*, thus codifying doctrines to which they subscribe even today.

dGe lugs pa School

By this time Buddhism in one form or another had permeated the whole of Tibetan society. There was hardly any Tibetan who did not acknowledge Buddhism as the guiding principle of his life. Those who called themselves *Bon po* too subscribed to identical religious beliefs and attitudes even if they called them by other names.

The *dGe lugs pa* school was the last of the Buddhist schools to come into being. It was founded by a renowned saint called Tsong kha pa (1357-1419 A.D). He exerted far more lasting influence on Buddhism in Tibet than any

16. Ibid.

other saint. With the emergence of this school Buddhism in Tibet can be said to have found its final form.

The name *dGe lugs pa* means "Followers of the Way of Virtue". To the Westerners this school is known as the Yellow Hat school from the colour of the head-dress of its adherents.

Tsong kha pa

Tsong kha pa was born in the neighbourhood of the great lake of Kokonor in the northern part of Tibet. As a young man he travelled from monastery to monastery in Central Tibet, studying under teachers of different schools. At the age of forty he joined the bKa' gdams pa monastery at Rva sgrengs and became a religious teacher. He preached the ideals of monastic discipline and insisted on celibacy and abstention from intoxicants. His religious views were based on the works of great Indian philosophers like Nāgārjuna, Asaṅga, Diṅnāga, and Āryadeva. He expounded his views in the way of Mahāyāna Buddhism in a work entitled "The Great Exposition of the Stages of the Way". He founded his own monastery called dGa' ldan in 1409 A.D., near Lhasa. Later, with support from a number of monks of the older schools as well as lay people, his disciples established two more monasteries in the vicinity of Lhasa - Dre spungs in 1416 A.D., and Se ra in 1419 A.D.

In 1408 A.D., Tsong kha pa instituted the annual New Year celebrations in the ancient Jo khang Temple in Lhasa, intending them as a yearly rededication of Tibet to Buddhism. The congregational prayer that was offered on the occasion was known as the Great Prayer. This Great Prayer was offered every year till 1959.

Tsong kha pa's own learning and the strictly regulated and austere religious life of his monks secured popular support for his school. This utterly eclipsed the work and influence of the bKa gdams pa school, which consequently ceased its separate existence. Although Tsong kha pa emphasized the early non-*tantric Mahāyāna* philosophy, he composed commentaries on the *tantras* and found for them a place at the highest level of monastic studies. Eventually two *dGe lugs pa* monasteries specially devoted to *tantric* studies were established in Lhasa for mastering the "upper" and the "lower" tantras. These monasteries drew elite monks who were subjected to an extremely rigorous code of discipline in their studies, thus elevating *tantric* studies to a high, sacred pedestal and dispelling the popular notion that practitioners of the tantras were a corrupt and degenerate lot in Tibet.[17] Tsong kha pa was known as a great reformer of Buddhism in Tibet. The school he founded, under the name of *dGe lugs pa,* represented the reformed sect, encompassing all that was conductive to the maintenance and growth of the sacred order.

A common feature of all the schools in Tibet, one which linked them to the other schools of Asia, was their adoption of the same *Vinaya* code on the ordination and regulation of daily life. Superimposed on this basic code were the diverse curricula which served to distinguish Tibetan monks from most of their neighbours to the east and southeast. It was the *tantric* orientation of the curricula which made them typically Tibetan. Almost all of the art and music and most of the literature found in the Tibetan monasteries were the product of the complex ritual cycles which were part of monastic life in Tibet.

---

17. Ibid., p.264.

Conflicts between the Schools

The different schools outlined above represented all the important trends and tendencies that were in evidence in Tibetan Buddhism. One could discern in them a compromise between the Indian tradition and the indigenous liturgical and mythological heritage. Together the different schools and their work constituted the world of Lamaism in all aspects. The schools even intervened in the political life of the country in a decisive manner.

Monastic organizations took the place of the landholding aristocracy or allied themselves with them. The power of the abbots replaced that of the hereditary feudal nobility. The monasteries became economic and political organizations too. Sometimes they opposed one another; sometimes they acted in concert to gain specific ends, as also to guard their independence. Increasingly the aristocracy became the secular arm of the monastic order. The two had common interests; and religious differences were used just as though they were a means of advancing those interests. The impulse towards domination came first from Byang chub rgyal mtshan (d.1373 A.D). This monk belonged to the family of Phag mo mgon pa, which owed allegiance originally to the *bKa' rgyud pa* school as already mentioned and was also closely connected with the *bKa' gdams pa* and *Sa skya pa* schools. These schools developed rather rapidly into major powers. They assigned the hereditary office of governor of the territories they had conquered (*rdzong dpon*) to certain families which had assisted them in their rise to power. Their hegemony, however, was restricted to Central Tibet. West Central Tibet not only remained outside their reach but also opposed their attempts to establish their dominance by siding with the *Karma pa* school. The conflict between Central Tibet and West Central Tibet was an important feature of Tibetan history for full two centuries with a steadily growing circle of leading families favouring one faction or another. Meanwhile the *dGe lugs pa* sect was able to consolidate its position, and bSad nams rgyal mtsho (1543-88 A.D). succeeded in converting the Mongol followers of Altai Khan to the Buddhist faith. What was more, the institution of Dalai Lama came into being.[18]

Dalai Lamas

With the emergence of the institution of Dalai Lama the history of Buddhism in Tibet became largely a history of the *dGe lugs pa* school and its rise to power. When a question of succession arose within the school, the *dGe lugs pa* school followed the model of the *Karma pa* school : it chose to settle the question of succession by relying on the popular belief in reincarnation. dGe 'dun grub (1391-1475 A.D.), Tsong kha pa's nephew, was also his successor twice removed. He was an energetic and ambitious leader. One of his first acts was to set about building a monastery in honour of Tsong kha pa, who had taught him during his formative period. He laid deep foundations for the building of the monastery and the surrounding walls and also took care to propitiate the local gods; for even the reformed *dGe lugs pa* did not dare to slight the old *Bon* beliefs too openly. This monastery was called *bKra shis lhun po*, or Mountain of Blessings. In the subsequent centuries it became the seat of the Panchen Lama, second only in rank to the Dalai Lama. dGe 'dun grub's successor was found in a child born soon after his death and recognized as his reincarnation. He was regarded as the second Dalai Lama,

18. Tucci, n.11, p.41

or Ocean of Wisdom, dGe 'dun grub being the first retrospectively. (The title was first bestowed on his immediate successor, bSad nams rgyal mtsho by Altai Khan, chief of the Mongols, in 1578 A. D.), Altai Khan felt so impressed by his holiness and serenity and power that he was converted to Buddhism. He tried to supress bloody sacrifices and the worship of ancestral images in Mongolia. All Mongolia accepted the *dGe lugs pa* school and adopted Tibetan Buddhism with all its rituals, texts, and art as its national religion. It, further, made literary Tibetan its sacred language. Mongol support for the *dGe lugs pa* school was strengthened when Dalai Lama IV was discovered in a great-grandson of Altai Khan's. Dalai Lama V won a final victory over his opponents - in particular, the King of gTsang and the *Karma pa* school - with the help of Gusri Khan, the leader of the Qoshot Mongols, who were settled in the Kokonor region. This brought him recognition as the undisputed master of Tibet. Subsequently, however, he showed considerable generosity towards other schools.

Dalai Lama V---Ngag dbang blo bzang rgyal mtsho--- is known to the Tibetans as the Great Fifth inasmuch as he was an unusually intelligent, strong-willed, and generous-minded ruler. He travelled to Beijing at the invitation of the Chinese Emperor, and the meeting between the two in 1655 A.D., was one between two equal heads of State. Lhasa became the centre of Tibet, symbolized by the magnificent Potala Palace, which the Dalai Lama had built on the foundations of the earlier constructions. The choice of the name "Potala" was significant; for it was the name of the mountain in South India which was regarded as the seat of Tibet's patron *Bodhisattva Avalokiteśvara*. The Great Fifth, being a reincarnation of his predecessor, is also believed to have been a manifestation of *Avalokiteśvara* like all the other Divine Kings. Two types of incarnation thus came to be united in one person for the first time. They have remained so down to the present Dalai Lama - Dalai Lama XIV.

During the regime of Dalai Lama V the prestige of the *dGe lugs pa* school increased further with the appearance of a second supreme spititual dignitary - the Panchen Lama. According to tradition, this dignitary was a reincarnation of *Amitābha* or God of Infinite Light. The *dGe lugs pa* school now claimed three supreme dignitaries as its own : the Dalai Lama, the Panchen Lama, and the grand abbot of dGa' ldan.

While the *dGe lugs pa* school enjoyed great privileges, the other sects were allowed to live in peace. Their monasteries too continued to grow or decline according to the degree of support they received from their respective adherents. Though certain schools like the *rNying ma pa* school enjoyed less popularity in many parts of Tibet in the subsequent centuries, yet it was true that everybody was free to follow any school according to his convictions.

The differences between the various schools were not very significant. They arose for the most part over certain specific features of the method of attaining salvation, or their theoretical premises, or their preference in favour of particular *tantras,* or their interpretations of the texts relating to, or experiences flowing from adherence to, particular *tantras.* The heads of the various schools were agreed that such differences should never be allowed to affect the unity of the faith. The multiplicity of opinions was to be understood as the coexistence of equally valid paths. One might find a certain path easier

19. Per Kvaerne, n.1, p.265.

to negotiate and another not so easy or convenient; or one might find a particular path straight and another indirect. All, however, led to the same goal, viz. liberation from suffering. Furthermore, it was held that each individual in this life chose the path that was the best and the most suitable. Everybody was guided in such a choice by *karmic* conditions which determined one's greater or less spiritual maturity, one's higher or lower ability to understand and actualize the supreme truths taught by the Buddha.[20]

The *rNying ma pa* school and the *Bon po* had nothing to fear under *dGe lugs pa* domination. For one thing they did not have any political ambitions or pretensions. Second, their centres of religious practice were generally small; there was little to destroy, and there was hardly anything worth taking away. It is, however, significant that the main *Bon po* centres developed in the far east of Tibet, in Amdo and rGyal rong, where they continued to operate as local monasteries and small teaching centres till the 1950s. Neither they nor the adherents of the *rNying ma pa* school suffered much at the hands of those of the *dGe lugs pa* school. In contrast the *Jo nang pas* were wiped out, and their chief monastery was converted into a *dGe lugs pa* monastery.[21]

The death of Dalai Lama V was kept a closely guarded secret for thirteen years, till 1695 A.D. Exactly two hundred years passed before another strong Dalai Lama emerged to play a decisive role in the destiny of Tibet. During the period the system of Government and religion and social life in Tibet remained practically

---

20. Tucci, n.11, p.43.
21. Samten G.Karmay, A Gernal Introduction to the History and Doctrines of Bon (Tokyo, 1985), p.186.

unchanged, except for some pressures and interventions from neighbouring Powers. In 1911 Dalai Lama XIII (1876-1934), who was a forceful personality, ended the patron- priest relationship between the Chinese Emperor and the Dalai Lama and re-established Tibet's complete independence from China. The Chinese garrison in Lhasa was expelled, and Tibet enjoyed full freedom till 1951. In the autumn of 1950 the Communist regime in China sent its army into Tibet. The Chinese overcame the organized resistance put up by the Tibetans. Dalai Lama XIV, bsTan dzin rgyal mtsho (b.1935), was hastily invested with full powers as head of State at the age of sixteen. However, resistance to Chinese rule increased year by year. Finally, in 1959, there was an uprising. When it failed, Dalai Lama XIV fled to India along with thousands of his followers.

Lama or Religious Teacher

The lama (*bla ma*), or teacher, in Tibetan Buddhism is very important inasmuch as he is considered a manifestation of the Buddha and thus entitled to transmit the teaching to his disciples as also to initiate them into esoteric doctrines. In a way Lamaism is a continuation of the Indian *Mahāyāna* tradition as it places the figure of the teacher at the core of the spiritual exercise.[22] As we have seen, the teacher in *Mahāyāna* and *Vajrayāna* Buddhism, through direct living contact/ transmits the teaching, in letter and in spirit, and kindles the spark which grows in time into the blazing fire of mystical experience. The bond between teacher and disciple is like the relationship between a father and his son but of a spiritual kind (*thugs sras*). As such it is incomparably

22. Tucci, n.11, pp.44.

more important than the bond of a mere blood relationship. If the teaching is transmitted down the centuries regularly from teacher to disciple, then it is called a *sampradāya* in India and *brgyud* in Tibet. Both the teacher and the disciple in a *sampradāya* then become links in a chain which guarantees the continued ascendancy of the teaching and the living power of the mystical experience. Word (*lung*) and power (*dbang*) come down over the tide of time in indissoluble unity. Not only does an instruction based simply on the written word without the participation of the teacher become ineffective but it also leads those concerned away from the right path and destroys them. Two functions are thus combined in the teacher. The teacher transmits the word, or passes on the teaching. What is more, he confers power through initiation or consecration. In special cases a teaching may be transmitted through a dream or by direct communication with the deity concerned.

There are two sides to be distinguished in Lamaism. There is, first, the world of religion, of monasteries and hermits, interested according to school or inclination in doctrine or liturgy, or in ascetic practices, or in *yoga*. Each man practices the teaching and performs appropriate rites in conformity with the rules prescribed therefor through initiation into mystical experience. The other side is concerned with the lay world, which, though outside such a communal life, is yet linked with it in the closest possible manner, breathing the same religious and spiritual air. Except for the vows relating to monastic discipline, which are meant exclusively for the monks, the laymen are bound by the same discipline. They are conjured to accumulate merit, worship the three jewels (viz. the

23. Ibid., p.45.

Buddha, the teaching, and the community), and take refuge in them and strive for supreme enlightenment. Though one may not obtain the mystical experience which is accessible only to those who have embraced the monastic life and received ordination, yet the life of a layman is not a life wasted from the spiritual point of view. It is a preparation, as it were, for the life to come and for the attainment of paradise. Though the taking of initiatory vows and compliance with traditional disciplinary procedures distinguish the life of a monk from that of a layman, yet certain ethical norms sanctified by tradition in the form of five abstentions (viz. from killing, stealing, speaking falsehood, committing adultery, and partaking of intoxicating drinks) are valid equally and without exception for both layman and monk.[24]

Common Doctrines of the Most Important Schools of Tibetan Buddhism

In spite of their differences, all schools are agreed in respect of many doctrinal matters.[25] The reality of suffering and man's desire to overcome suffering and to reach the state referred to as liberation constitute the fundamental premise. Liberation implies attainment of omniscience. It implies the overthrow of the plain of illusory experience and the attainment of a state in which omniscience, truth, and reality merge together. The perception of the true nature of appearances or illusory existence can eliminate imperfections which obstruct the way to liberation. The most important means to liberation is adherence to the Law (*Chos*) revealed by the Buddha. One who accepts the Law must be clearly aware of its true meaning and bring the individual ethical, cognitive,

24. Ibid., p.46..
25. Ibid., p.47.

and meditative elements together into a harmonious blend. Only then can he reach the desired goal. The final objective is to awaken that higher cognition (*shes rab*) in one's consciousness and to examine the ultimate nature of all things with the clarity of direct insight.

The Tibetan Buddhist view of the world has four elements : (1) Everything is connected with everything else; nothing has individual permanence. (2) All things and all concepts (except those arising from the Buddhist faith) are the causes and consequences of suffering and are indissolubly bound up with suffering. They continually give new nourishment to suffering in that they cause and promote the continuation of existence. (3) All things and all concepts that we regard as real till we attain spiritual and intellectual maturity are without true existence. Moreover, they are relative to one another and, therefore, "void". (4) There exists a state beyond suffering and beyond the world of appearances, and such a state is called *nirvāṇa*. *Nirvāṇa* is beyond description; it is beyond ordinary existence and also beyond that state of peaceful detachment which one attains in certain moments of meditation. It is the supreme, irreversible identification with the state which is called *Buddhahood*.

FIrst one takes refuge in the Buddha, the teching, and the community - i.e. at the start of the *Bodhi* path. This must be followed by an awakening within oneself of constant energy and its application to the fulfilment of the obligations which have arisen from the recognition of the fourfold truth, obligations both concerning what must be done and what must be renounced. Next one must resolve to overcome the world of relativity, suffering, and impermanence and take the vow to strive for enlightenment. The vow is not just in respect of one's personal salvation, a characteristic of *Hīnayāna*, but also in respect of the salvation of others, a characteristic of *Mahāyāna.* This represents the second revelation of the doctrine as condensed in the form of the *Phar phyin* scriptures. This stage is followed by the revelation of the gnostic magical vehicle, the vehicle of *sNgags* (*mantra*), also called *rDo rje theg pa* or the Diamond Vehicle (*Vajrayāna*). This division into vehicles is based on the construction of the path in terms of successive stages in accordance with the moral, intellectual, and karmic qualifications of the initiates.

According to the *Mādhyamika* school the assumption of a correct view is implicitly contained in the *Phar phyin* scriptures and placed by Nāgārjuna at the centre of the entire system. All that can be thought and known is relative and void and hence not a being-in-itself. Firm belief in this becomes an experience in five phases : (1) The phase of "accumulation of virtue" and of the overcoming of moral and intellectual defilements; (2) the phase of putting into practice of the truth postulated by *Mahāyāna,* i.e. the path to be followed to achieve Buddhahood, that final stage to which the thought of enlightenment should lead us; (3) the phase of vision; (4) the phase of meditative refinement;[26] and (5) the phase which gradually leads to the tenth "earth", a phase in which all defiments are dissolved and the attainment of Buddahood is irreversibly accomplished.

In addition to the above there is the vehicle of the *tantras.* It is said that the Buddha preached not only at Both Gaya (*Hīnayāna*) and the Vulture Peak (*Mahāyāna*) but also elsewhere, both on this earth and in the worlds of bliss. And it is not only the Buddha that is Śākyamuni but also other, equally evolved, holy men such as Vairocana and Samantabhadra. They have all revealed

26. Ibid., p.50.

the way that leads to salvation. They have given not only the revelation recorded in the *Phar phyin* scriptures but also the esoteric formulae (*sngags*) or the *tantras*. Esoteric wisdom does not give us intellectual perception, but an exalted, ecstatic consciousness. The actualization of this consciousness is aided by liturgical ceremonies having the power to release the emotional impulses capble of renovating and transforming the individual so that he might proceed step by step and attain to a higher plane of existence. The literature conerning this process and the actions preserbed there for are wrapped in secrecy and hidden from non-initiates. There is, therefore, an imperative need for initiation and to ocercome inborn or acquired ignorance and to eliminate every conceivable dichotomy. The *tantras* revealed by the Enlightened Ones and transmitted through direct teaching from master to disciple help in this process. This path has an advantage over the Way of *Phar phyin* or the way of rationality in that while the latter requires an extremely long period of time for the attainment of the goal, the former offers the shortest path. In other words, whereas the followers of *Phar phyin* require several lives to attain Buddhahood, those who follow the *tantras* achieve it within a single life-time.[27]

In sum, Buddhism was officially introduced into Tibet in the seventh century A.D., in the reign of King Srong brtsan sgam po. The motives of this King in accepting Buddhism were more political than religious. Of course we cannot entirely rule out the possibility of Buddhist teaching having penetrated into Tibet earlier, off and on, by various routes from Central Asia, or from China, or from Nepal. The teaching that came to Tibet was significantly different from the doctrine preached by

27. Ibid., p.55.

Śākyamuni. It was *Mahāyāna* as propounded by Nāgārjuna, with his doctrine of *śūnyatā*, together with the later innovations of *vajrayāna*. Along with Buddhism the country also received a literary language. Althouth Buddhism entered Tibet under Royal patronage, it did not find the going easy on account of opposition from eertain powerful noble families which felt their privileges threatented. These powerful noble families combined with the *Bon po* against Buddhism, and consequently a conflict ensued. The *Bon po* armed themselves with a doctrinal and philosophical structure on Buddhist lines while the Buddhist assimlated the local deities and rituals into their religion in order to make themselves acceptable to the local people.

There was also a conflict between the Chinese and Indian forms of Buddhism. This led to a great debate in the reign of Khri srong lde brtsan in the eighth century. Eventually the Indian form found acceptance, and the Chinese form was banished.

As for the clnflict between *Bon* and Buddhism, both suffered. Buddhism suffered a setback in the wake of the end of the Royal dynasties. The country itself disintegrated and was plunged into darkness for nearly a century and a half. There is hardly any record relating to this period of darkness.

Buddhism was, however, revived in the eleventh century, thanks to the efforts of monks and selfless teachers, while it disappeared from India, the land of its birth, in the face of invasions by Muslims from other countries. A number of schools of Buddhism emerged under learned teachers, the last of such schools being the *dGe lugs pa* school with its well-organized monastiries, its elibate monks, and its pure monastic life by teachers and pupils under the leadership of the Dalai Lama.

All along, translations of Indian Buddhist texts were carried out from Sanskrit into Tibetan on a large scale. This culminated in the compliation of the Tibtan Buddhist canon, the *bKa' 'gyur* and the *bStan 'gyur*, in the founteenth century A.D.

Meanwhile the *Bon po* too organized themselves on Buddhist lines, partly by copying Buddhist texts and partly by learning the Buddhist doctrine and adapting it, along with their own material, to their requirements. The result was the emergence of a systematized *Bon* tradition with its own philosophical and doctrinal literature. The *Bon po* too organized a monastic order. They compiled their own bKa' 'gyur, the words of Master gShen rab mi bo, who was their Buddha, and their own bStan 'gyur, the learned commentaries on those words by subseqent scholars.

The two traditions thus coexisted and gave Tibet its unique religious culture as expressd in its monasteries, shrines, sculptures, paintings, and icons and, above all. in the day-to- day life of its people.

CHAPTER SEVEN

Conclusion

Bon and Buddhism have existed side by side in Tibet since the seventh century and given that country a unique religious culture, which is reflected in its monasteries, temples, and shrines and in its sacred art and in its icons based on religious motifs. Religion predominates in Tibet: most of its people are either *Bon po* or Buddhists. *Bon* represents the pre-Buddhist religion (or religions) of Tibet. It has developed in historical times under the stimulus and inspiration provided mainly by the introduction of Buddhism. If it has borrowed or absorbed a vast amount of Buddhist lliterature, beliefs, and practices, it has also given to Buddhism much of its ritual, as well as gods and goddesses. According to David, L.Snellgrove,[1] "*Bon* and Buddhism in Tibet are in their theories and practices one and the same." The Tibetans practise both religions as moral and spritual disciplines.

When Buddhism first appeared in Tibet in the seventh century A.D., it found a flourishing system of popular beliefs and practices which people called *Bon*. Buddhism gradually absorbed some of these religious practices. This helped the newly converted people psychologically and facilitated the change from the old

---

1. David L.Snellgrove, *Nine Ways of Bon* (Boulder, Colo.,1980), p.13.

beleifs to the new. It provided the basis, so to say, for the development of a new culture that is the exclusive contribution of Tibet to world cuture.

The Buddhists constitute the vast majority of the people of Tibet although they are divided into a number of schools and sects. The *Bon po* are relatively few. They are concentrated in Amdo and Kham and in the Himalayan region. Even in Central Tibet, which is the stronghold of a school of Buddhism called the *dGe lugs pa* school, they have monasteries with several hundreds monks living in them. Both the *Bon po* and the Buddhists call themselves *nang pa*, or insiders, as against all foriegners such as the Indians, the chinese and the Europeans, who are *phyi pa*, or outsiders. The small number of Christians and Muslims are also known as *phyi pa*. *Bon po* and Buddhist monks have the same patterns of faith, study, and monastic life. Both call the founders of their respective religions *Sangs rgyas* or Buddha. Both aim at the attainment of *byang chub* (which means, literally, awakening, the same as "*bodhi*" in Sanskrit) and by using identical means. An investigation of *Bon* and Buddhism in the form in which we find them today would show that they are alike. They are, according to Tibetan culture, lamaistic.[2]

As explained in Chapter III, *Bon* grew out of nature worship by a simple people. With the entry of Buddhism it developed gradually into an advanced system of beliefs and parctices. The term "Bon" according to its adheraults, significs the highest and ultimate principle. Its cosmology divides the world into two spheres---the visible and the invisible. The visible sphere consists of the physical world of man with its animals and celestial beings; the invisible

---

2. Per kvaerne, "The Genesis of Tibetan Buddhist Tradition", Tibetan Review (New Delhi), March 1976, p.9.

sphere comprises supernatural forces---a hierarchy of divinities and demons who dwell in the cosmic realm. These forces represent both the good amd the evil which govern a man's conduct, reflecting their strengths and their weaknesses. Man stands at the centre of the interplay of these cosmic forces.

In the *Bon* religion the timely and proper performance of sacramental worship and propitiatory rites as prescribed by oracles is an effective means of placating the cosmic forces and of enlisting their help in curing an illness or in warding off a storm or in subduing an enemy, or in relieving drought. To ignore oracles and to fail to maintain harmony within oreself and with nature is to provoke the wrath of the divinities and to bring down natural calamities upon the community. In short, consistency of belief in the reality of the heavenly powers and in the exercise of moral discrimination, togather with a conscious performance of the various prescribed duties so as to resist the temptations offered by the evil forces rooted in oneself, carries rewards. Man is not just an aggregate of material elements and forces. He is a spiritual being with an inherent potential to rise above the mundane affairs of thes world.[3]

The Tibetans passionately believe in the interdependence of man and nature. They regard the earth as sacred, and a non-exploitative releationship between man and nature as necessary. Fear of upsetting nature's balance makes them ensure that rivers, streams, amd lakes are not polluted and that the earth does not bear deep scars of mining. This belief predates the advent of Buddhism in Tibet. It has survived the decline in the

3. Lobsang Lhalungpa, "The Religious Culture of Tibet", Tibet Journal (Dharamsala), vol.1, nos 3-4, autumn 1976, pp. 9-11.

dominance of *Bon* and is a part of the present-day culture of Tibet. There are number of other pre-Buddhist customs and symbols too in Tibetan culture. For example, the ancient belief in the sanctity of the kitchen and the hearth and the roof top persists in Tibet even today. The burning of incense and juniper boughs is a regular feature. The people also take care not to offend the resident sorpent gods. The walls continue to be decorated just as in the old days with auspicious figures and signs representing different deities. Butter sculpture is yet another important part of *Bon* and Buddhist ceremonies in Tibet. The prolific prayer fiags adapted for Buddhist use previously carried imprints of the *rlung ta* or the wind horse, the symbol of four elements, whcih represents the energy of the pure spirit.[4] The simple fact, however, is that these ancient pre-Buddhst forms and patterns of thought survive in Buddhist customs even at the present day.

For the Buddhists of Tibet, their Buddha is Śākyamuni who lived in India in the sixth century BC. The Buddha of the *Bon po* is sTon pa gShen rab who is said to have lived much before Śākyamuṇi in the country of sTag gzig which lies to the west or northwest of Tibet. (According to them, gShen rab was born as Buddha later in India.) They maintain that it was gShen rab who brought the teaching of the Buddha from sTag gzig to the country of Shang shung which, they say, was situated in the northern or northwestern part of Tibet and which included the area surrounding Mount *Ti se*. From Shang shung the doctrine travelled to Tibet, and the Tibetans translated the holy texts from the language of Shang shung into their own language. *Bon* was well established in Tibet when the Buddhist faith first appeared there. It was,

4. Ibid.

thanks to Royal patronage, that Buddhism was able gradually to supplant *Bon*. Consequently a bitter struggle followed between the Buddhists who enjoyed Royal protection, and the *Bon po* who had the support of powerful aristocratic familes. The result was the end of the Royal dynasties. With the dynasties gone, the country was plunged into a state of chaos in which both the *Bon po* and the Budddists suffered. It was about the year A.D. 1000 that the country emerged from the crisis under a politically powerful Buddhist hierarchy connected with large monastic centres. Simultaneously there appeared an organized tradition whose followrs called themselves *Bon po* but who were manifestly Buddhist.[5] According to Snellgrove,[6] the development of *Bon* and Buddhism and the proliferation of their literature have been parallel processes. Both have used the same literary language within the same cultural milieu. Naturally, therefore, the literature of the one is much the same as that of the other. Nonetheless even a glance at *Bon po* literature should suffice to convince us of its dependence on Buddhist literature. The *Bon po* have copied especially their *sūtra* and the teaching about the Perfection of Wisdom from the litrature of the Buddhists. By far the greater part has, however, been absorbed through learning and then reproduced along with their own material according the their requirements. It would not be fair to dub it plagiarism, given the exceptionally keen desire of the *Bon po* to study and imbibe the best in the teaching of the other tradition.

On the doctrinal plane there has been no real opposition between the two religions. Nor have their relations been always hostile to each other. Contemporary

5. Per Kvaerne,n.2, pp.10-12.
6. Snellgrove,n.1, p.13.

sources show that there were conflicts when *Bon po* monasteires were burnt down and its followers persecuted, but there never was any planned or organizaed persecution. In fact the worst happened to the other tradition. The *Jo nang pa* sect of Buddhism, for example, was subjected to persecution, and all its monasteries were forcibly closed down in the seventeenth century A.D. by Dalai Lama V.Ties between the *Bon po* and the adherents of the *rNying ma pa* school have been particularly close in view of the doctrinal similarities between the two, especially in the field of *rDzogs chen* or the Great Perfection teaching. In fact a number of impartial scholars take *Bon* and Buddhism "almost as two aspects" of an identical religion.

The similarities between *Bon* and Buddhism can best be illustrated with reference to their religious practices. To begin with, there is the manner in which the Bon po have formulated their triad.[7] It is so similar to the Buddhist triad.

	Buddhism	**Bon**
(1)	***dKon mchog gsum*** **("Rare perfect Three")**	**gYung-drung gsum ("Swastika Three")**
(2)	***dKon mchog dge 'dun*** **("Rare Perfect Virtuous Assembly or Community")**	**gYung-drung sems dpa'a ("Swastika Hero Mind")**
(3)	***dKon mchog chos*** **("Rare Perfect Law")**	***gYung-drung bon*** **("Swastika Bon")**

In formulating the triad the *Bon po* have accepted *Sangs rgyas* ("Buddhahood") as the first entity, but have

7. Robert B.Ekval, Religious Observances in Tibet (Chicago, Ill., 1964),p.23.

linked it to the *swastika* concept expressed as gYung-drung *Sangs rgyas*. Their *swastika*, however, is only a symbol. The concept is defined as the unchangeable and the permanent or the everlasting!

Ekval makes an in-depth study of the practices of the two religions and identifies the rites and observances which are commom---in such fields as (1) the pantheon, (2) magic, (3) prayers, and (4) offerngs. Except for minor differences of intent, aspect or emphasis, the two religoins have many things in common.[8]

Let us, for example, take the pantheon first. Most of it is shared by the two religions. It can be comprehensively summed up in the Tibetan bipartite term *lHa 'Dre*, or god-goblin, which clearly reflects a dualistic concept of existence. Another system suggests a tripartite view of the cosmos, thus: (1) those above the *lHa,* or the gods: (2) those of the middle region, viz. the *sa bdag,* or the earth lords and/or the gNyan or the strong ones; and (3) those of the nether world, viz. the *klu,* or the serpent spirits. The first of these systems is probably *Bon* in origin, and the other seems to be Buddhist. Cutting across these systems of classification is their division into categories of three, five, eight, nine, twelve, thirteen, and so on up to three hundred and sixty. One cannot tell, however, which gods and demons belong to which category; for the categories overlap and contain duplicates or differing aspects of the same spirit or spirits. This has been particularly evident since the time of Padmasambhava, when a number of indigenous demons were converted and subjugated to Buddhism so that, instead of being the implacable enemeis of that religion, they became *Chos* skyong or protectors or guardians of Buddhism.

8. Ibid., pp. 24-29.

In the face of the problem of existence and the inherited belief in a vast pantheon of spirit beings who are either beneficent or malignant, both the *Bon* religion and Tibetan Buddism have accepted magic as an essential component. Not only has Buddhism borrowed magic from *Bon*, but its own *tantric* school founded by Padmasmbhava believes in magic and is greatly preoccupied with the problem of controlling and manipulating spirits by means of ritualistic posturing, incantations, and spells. Magic is accordingly an important part of the services that the two religions---*Bon* and Buddhism---offer to the Tibetan community. There may be differences in the manner in which such services are offered and in the uses to which they are put. Even the monks of the *dGe lugs pa* school practise magic on request though with some reluctance. The reluctance is due to the fact that they deprecate the need to use magic and would rather rely on their doctrine. Those of the *rNying ma pa* school are more ready to use magic. However, it is the *Bon po* who are specialists in the use of magic. The orthodox *Bon* monks bless individuals and communities, pronounce protective spells against evil, combine magic with the administration of herbal medicine in healing physical ailments, and forctell the futhure for those who ask. But these are matters of detail. The fact is that magic is common to both religions.

Prayer too is a part of both religions. Most verbal expressions of the religious feeling are borrowed from each other so that it is difficult to distinguish between the *Bon po* and the Buddhists; and, when merely heard, they could be taken as belonging to either system. The rythmic repetition of the syllables in measured movement and in a special tone, accompained by a characteristic play on percussion and wind instruments, is common to the two. Of course there are specific manifestations of the religious utterance which can, if carefully heard, be recognized as belonging to the one or the other of the two religions. However, such manifestations are rare; and, when they do occur, they only underline the basic differences which the borrowings have not influenced.

As for offerings, they range from incense, flowers, grain, pure water, lights and music to the use of the *maṇḍala*. Both the *Bon po* and the Buddhists make offerings which consist of images or emblems shaped from dough, butter, or other similar substances and which, according to the ritual or incantations, become the containers of bad luck or bearers of retribution. Depending on the nature of the ceremony, they are later either burned or broken up and thrown away. This type of offering points to the practice of sacrificing live animals by the *Bon po* in the past. Animal sacrifice was forbidden in the time of Padmasambhava in the eighth century. Instead people were exhorted to use images made of dough or butter as substitutes.

Although the *Bon po* claim that their religion is in line with the original doctrine of the Buddha, Hoffman says that often it negates Buddhism. Ekval even speaks of wilful distorions or perversions of Buddhist ritual---as, for example, counterclockwise cirumambulation in a place of worship (an important religious practice in both religions). However, Per Kvaerne, who was personally acquainted with a number of *Bon po*, both monks and laymen, and who had access to texts of all kinds. feels otherwise. He concedes that the *Bon po* texts contain a good deal of material that is not Buddhist, but that this is true of the Buddhist texts too. He found in the *Bon po* an exceptional willingness to learn and study the teaching of the other tradition. As for circumambulation, Professor Tucci says:

Even one of the characteristic precepts of the Bon religion, the anti-clockwise circummambulation (which was in any case not unkwown to the Buddhists: it was practised with respect to *Saṁvara*), could be transformed into its opposite; at a later period the *Bon po* too took over the clockwise movement (*gYas skor*) and in this case they also clearly took into account the doctrinal principles with which it was connected. The clockwise circling was regarded as the circle of the means (*Thabs skor*) and the ante clockwise as the circle of transcendent consciousness (*ye gShes skor*). Another principle of division was also used and in some rituals the clockwise circumambulation was reserved for man and called "sun circling" while the anti-clockwise or "moon circling" was reserved for women.

This leaves hardly any difference between the two traditions as regards this important religious practice.

Tucci also mentions that just as the Buddhists distinguish three or four bodies or three or four or five phases of illusory life in its manifestation and revelation, the *Bon po* accept five bodies: *Bon sku* (*Dharmakāya* of the Buddhists); *Longs sku* (*Saṁbhogakāya*); *Sprul sku* (Nirmāṇakāya); *aNgo bo nyid* (*Svābhāvikakāya*); and *Mngon byang* (body of enlightenment).[9]

Both *Bon* and Buddhism accord fundamental importance to light. Both regard it as a generative principle, as a symbol of the ultimate reality. Everythig comes out of light. Light is present in everybody. In the *Bon po* theory of creation of the universe, from the pure undifferentiated light were born a black light and a white light. From the black light there came a black man; and from the white light, a white man. The black man

9. Giuseppe Tucci, Religions of Tibet (New Delhi, 1980), pp.242- 3, See also Helmut Hoffman, The Religions of Tibet, Edward Fitzgerald, trans. (London, 1961),p.17; and Per Kvaerne, n.2.

represented the principle of negation, of non-being. He was the source of the demons and of drought. He also brought with him the pestilence and all kinds of misfortune. On the other hand the white man symbolized the positive principle and was the source of all that was good. That was how the twofold creation began. The supreme *Bon* divinity was gShen lha 'od-dkar, the white light. Blessings of saints were also conveyed through the luminous rays of light emanating from them. In the Buddhist literature dedicated to the technique of transformation of the life principle at the moment of death, the vision of light was a fundamental element. The consciousness of a spirtually mature person identified itself with the light that shone at the time of death; it perceived the identity between that light and its own radiant essence.[10]

We have already mentioned (in Chapter V) that when Guru Padmasambhava visited Tibet to subdue the deities inimical to Buddhism, he was victorious over all of them and spared their lives only after extracting a promise from them that they would thenceforth be protectors and defenders of the Buddhist Law. The deities he subdued included the local gods of mountains and rocks known as *'Dre, Srin, bTsan*, and so on; these consequently became common to both *Bon* and Buddhism. They possessed supernatural powers and were capable of working miracles. If they were offended in some manner or were discontented, their violent nature came to the fore. Many of them, however, were benevolent in nature and were ready to fight evil. These became *Bodhisattvas.* For instance, gNyan chen thang lha, a popular divine figure of the pre-Buddhist period, became a *Bodhisattva.* Similarly the planet *Rāhu* became a *Bodhisattva* of the

10. Tucci, n.9, pp. 63-64.

tenth "earth". Although these deities performed such basic magical operations as pacifying malevolent spirits and bringing good fortune, they were incapable of participation in facilitating the attainment of the highest goal, viz. salvation. This task was reserved for the supermundane gods. A number of gods were considered to have the power to become supermundane through spiritual purification. Those without such power remained worldly deities.[11]

Entry into the *Bon po* community was an important event in the life of an individual. Prior to that event a man went through a ritual in which he was administered the oath of relgious life. Any breach of the oath brought severe punishment. The principal part of the punishment was to threaten those guilty of any breach of word in the most terrible terms. This task was entrusted to certain special gods. These gods belonged to the class of *Dam chan* and formed part of the general class of *Chos skyong*. In Buddhism too such gods watched over the keeping of vows and were regarded as protective deities. All those who had taken the vow were called *mched*, or brothers. However, this fraternity was somewhat more than the assembly of the Buddhists. The religious ceremony in which the *Bon po* took part was a kind of sacrament, bringing about a state of brotherhood which lasted after the end of the ceremony too. In contrast the assembly was just a congregation brought together for the performance of any particular rite.[12]

Magic is common to both *Bon* and Buddhism as mentioned earlier. Rene de Nebesky-Wojkowitz, who has studied the various aspects of Tibetan religious life and practice, has found a number of traditions in both *Bon*

11. Ibid., p. 164.
12. Ibid., p. 240.

and Buddhism which clearly hark back to the early *Shamanistic* times. For instance, there is a close resemblance between a *Shaman* drum and *rnga chen*, or a drum beaten by means of a stick curved far back. *Bon* magicians are supposed to have used drums as vehicles for flying, which is a *Shamanistic* trait. According to a legend, gShen rab mi bo used to fly on a huge wheel. He used to install himself in the centre. His eight disciples used to sit around him, one on each of the eight spokes. It was the Buddhists who introducted the symbol of the eight-spoked wheel.

A number of common items were used ceremonially by the *Bon po*, the Buddhists, and the *Shamans* alike. For instance, a piece of felt was used for kneeling or spreading ceremonial items. Buddhist priests officiating as oracles used a felt hat; so did the *Shamans*. Also, they often used an arrow in the magic exercises like the *Shamans*. They covered their faces while performing a ceremony. Indeed it was a common characteristic of both the *Shamans* and the Buddhist oracles. The trances of the oracles corresponded in their intensity, as well as in their main features, to those of the *Shamans*.[13]

All these are examples of common traits of *Bon* and Buddhism. Such examples can be multiplied. Further, there are many important areas like *Vinaya* (i.e. monastic initiation and discipline), the education and training of monks, monastic vows and the like, where the two traditions follow the same practices. The aim of these religious observances is the same, viz. salvation. In broad terms the methods adopted for achieving this aim are similar. Procedures for the practice of meditation too are

13. Rene De Nebesky-Wojkowitz, Oracles and Demons of Tibet (The Hague, 1956), pp.538-48.

identical. For the Buddhists the ultimate reality is śūnyatā, whereas for the *Bon po* it is *Bonku*. All this indicates that there is no real opposition between *Bon* and Buddhism on the doctrinal plane, and there is little difference, execpt in matters of detail, in their religious observances. Snellgrove and Richardson regard the two traditions today as one. To quote them:

> Buddhism and *Bon* were mingled to the end. In the cathedral itself, the holiest Buddhist place in Tibet, a resident *Bon po* priest performed daily ceremonies, while on the roof a stack of junipur boughs was renewed every New Year in accordance with ancient *Bon* custom. The ancient family of lHa gya ri with its Royal connexions still had its *Bon po* chaplain, who performed the naming rites of its children and the funeral ceremonies of its dead, while the Tibetan Government sent an official every year to a chapel near the Yar lung Valley to burn butter-lamps and give grain to the birds, as an invitation to the cuckoo, the sacred bird of *Bon*, to return to Tibet.[14]

After the Lhasa uprising in 1959, large numbers of Tibetan - men, women, and childern - fled to India. With the help of the Government of India and several international organizations, refugee camps were established in different places on the Himalayan range and as far south as the State of Karnatka. It is estimated that the present number of Tibetan refugees in India and Nepal is about one hundred thousand. Approximately one per cent of this total (i.e. about a thousand) are *Bon po*.

The Buddhists have established themselves at Dharamsala with the Dalai Lama as their secular and temporal head. There they follow the same old religious practices and perform the same religious rites as have been laid down for the *dGe lugs pa* order. They have

14. David L.Snellgrove and Hugh E.Richardson, A Cultural History of Tibet (Boulder, Colo.,1980), p.267.

thus converted Dharamsala into a mini Tibet. The *Bon po* too have, after much struggle, established a monastic centre at Dolanji near Solan in Himachal Pradesh. The main purpose of this centre is the pursuit of a strict, monastic life and the education of monks in the performance of religious ceremonies. Other activities include the publication of *Bon po* texts, the painting of *thang ka*, the maintenance and administration of two medical dispensaries (one based on the traditional Tibetan system of medicine and the other following the allopathic system), the cultivation of a small piece of land, the construction of houses, and the dispatch of monks to help other *Bon po* groups in India and Nepal in their spiritual needs. The monastic centre is maintained solely with the help of voluntary donations and offerings received in return for the performance of religious ceremonies.[15]

This monastic community consists of three groups of men. The first group consists of monks who came from Tibet. Their main activities are the performance of religious ceremonies in the houses of laymen, private religious practices, and participation in all the rites which take place in the monastery. They include several monks who have, in their lives, followed the special methods of spiritual perfection according to the *rDzogs chen* and Buddhist traditions. There are also those who have taken their vows at this centre. They are being educated in the *Bon po* doctrines and trained to live according to *Bon po* monastic rules. Their basic education lasts about eight years, and it concludes with their completion of the *dGe bshes* examinations. If successful, they are awarded the dGe bshes degree, corresponding roughly to a doctrate

15. Tadeusz sKorupsky, "Tibetan gYung-drung Monastery at Dolanji", Kailash (Kathmandu), vol. 8, nos 1-2, 1981,p. 26.

in religion in universities based on the Western model. The syllabus consists of dialectics (*mTshan nyid*), logic (*Tshad ma*), the wisdom texts (Phar phyin), the gradual stages of inner progress (*Sa lam*), the philosophy of the Middle Path (*dBu ma*), cosmology, metaphysics (*mDzod phug*), monastic discipline(*'Dul ba*), *tantras* (*rGyud*), Great Perfection (*rDzogs chen*), history (*Chos byung*), poetry (*sDeb abyor*), astrology (*rTsis*), and Tibetan grammar. The third group in the monastery consists of boys between seven and fourteen years of age studying in the school set up by the Government of India. Outside school hours they take part in all ceremonies in the temple and receive instruction in religion, Tibetan calligraphy, painting, and religious music.

It would thus seem that the *Bon* tradition will continue and that it will maintain its own identity, which does not appear to be substantially different from that of Buddhism. There has no doubt been constant rivalry between the different schools of Buddhism as well. What is of fundamental importance to us is the basic doctrinal identity and the common cultural idiom between *Bon* and Buddhism; for these transcend borders and factional rivalries, uniting Tibetans into a Tibetan nation profoundly committed to religion.

In the end we may make brief mention of the *Ris med* movement, which seeks to unite the various religious schools on a common doctrinal basis, emphasizing beliefs and practices that are common to all traditions. "*Ris med*" means impartial or non-aligned or universal. This movement arose in the nineteenth century in *rNying ma pa* circles in Kham and influenced monks belonging to other schools. A typical product of this movement is the *Bon po* lama, bKra shis rgyal mtshan (1859-1935), from Shardza. Another is his pupil, the *dGe lugs pa* lama who became the abbot of the Brag dkar monastery in Kandze. This movement was under way when the Chinese intervention came and disrupted religious life totally in Tibet. It is, however, clear that the *Ris med* movement clearly indicates the direction in which Tibetan Buddhism "will have to evolve if it is to remain the 'ultimate concern' of future generations of Tibetans".[16]

---

16. Per Kvaerne, "Tibet : The Rise and Fall of a Monastic Tradition", in Heinze Bechart and Richard Gombrich, eds, The World of Buddhism (London, 1984), p.270.

Appendix

LIVING TRACES OF BON IN THE NORTHWEST HIMALAYA

Chapter IV of this book contains, among other things, an account of the significant contribution of Shang shung to the evolution and development of *Bon* in Tibet. According to tradition, gShen rab mi bo, the founder of the *Bon* religion, while on a visit to Tibet in search of his stolen horses, took the opportunity to preach *Bon* to the people of that country. However, not finding them ready to receive his teaching, he prophesied that one day, when the time was ripe, his teaching would come to Tibet from Shang shung. In those days the people of Tibet used to call *Bon* priests from Shang shung (from Bru sha, to be precise, which was a part of Shang shung) to perform burial rites for their dead, to cure illnesses, and to appease the various spirits so as to avert calamities. When in the eighth century A.D. *Bon* came face to face with Buddhism with its solid philosophical and doctrinal structure, the *Bon po* of Tibet invited *Bon* priests from Shang shung to put their religion too on a similar philosophical and doctrinal footing and enable it to face the challenge posed by the new religion.

It is now widely believed on the basis of certain traditions that Shang shung was an independent kingdom till the seventh or the eighth century A.D., when it was annexed to Tibet either by Srong brtsan sgam po or Khri srong lde brtsan. (The legends vary.) Shang shung reportedly occupied an enormous area comprising three different regions: *sGo ba*, the outer region; *Phug pa*, the inner region; and *Bar ba*, the middle region. The outer region extended from Bru sha in the west to Dangs ra khyung rdzong in the east, next to Lake *gNam mtsho*, and from Khotan in the north to Chu mig brgyad cu rtsa gnyis in the south; the inner region comprised sTag gzigs; and the middle region included rGya mkhar bar chod, a place not yet identified. It is not certain that Shang shung covered such a large area, but it appears to have covered the whole of West Tibet. What was more, it was an independent kingdom. Its capital was Khyung lung dngul mkhar, a town that lay to the west of Mount *Ti se*. According to ancient records, Shang shung included Pu hrangs (Purang), Gu ge, Ru thog (Rudok), Chu murti, Spy ti (Spiti), lHa yul (Lahaul), Zangs dkar (Zanskar), Mar yul, La dvags (Ladakh), Baltistan, and Bru sha. Even to this day these areas, with the exception of Bru sha., are Tibetan-speaking. In the course of the centuries, these areas were occupied by different tribes - viz. the Mons, the Dards, the Balties, and others---along with the Tibetans. And gradually, with the mingling of these tribes, these areas lost the nomadic element, and the various tribes acquired the status of settled communities.

It is said that prior to the introduction of Buddhism in Ladakh, the religion of the people of the western part of the Himalaya was *Bon*. It is also said that it was Ton pa gShen rab who founded the religion in the extreme

---

1. Samten G. Karmay, A General Introduction to the History and Doctrines of Bon (Tokyo, 1975), p.180.
2. A.H. Francke, A History of Western Tibet (New Delhi, 1977), p.18.

southwestern border regions of Tibet in Shang shung. From there, presumably, the religion gradually spread to Central Tibet, West China, Gāndhāra, and Mongolia. Although the salient points of the *Bon* faith as practised of yore in Ladakh are now forgotten, a few practices and rites are still in vogue both in the Ladakh area and in the Tibetan-speaking areas of Bhutan, India and Nepal. The practice of raising prayer flags on the tops of tents, the rites relating to the worship of snakes, and the cults centring on local deities - all hark back to the *Bon* religion. One also comes across a few *Bon po* families in Ladakh which still perform certain rites for the expulsion of evil. The services of the *Bon po* are indispensable in Buddhist funerals.[3]

Thus, in the Northwest Himalaya one can still find the pre- Buddhist religion, viz. *Bon*, coexisting with other religions, mainly Hinduism and Buddhism. To identify all the traces of *Bon* in the region one might need to make a full-fledged field study. Even then one might not get a good enough picture as the *Bon po* families resident in the region may not like to disclose their true identity in view of the contempt in which the Buddhists hold them for adhering to *Bon*. However, on the basis of the published information available we have attempted in the following pages a brief account of certain ancient beliefs, practices, and rites which appear to be *Bon* inspired. We have also made note of the carvings on rocks and the icons in some temples. We have relied for these data on district gazetteers, the accounts set down by some officers of the then British Government, and the travel records

---

3. Nawang Tsering, "A Survey of the Spread of Buddhadharma in Ladakh", in Barbara Nimri Aziz and Matthew Kapstein, eds, soundings in Tibetan Civilization (New Delhi, 1985), pp. 157-8.

of a number of foreign visitors in the late nineteenth and early twentieth centuries, as well as the history of the region as compiled by them. The foreign visitors include A.H.Francke, Heinrich Harrer, Snellgrove, sKorupsky, Cunningham, Thompson, and Michel Peissel.

Lahaul and Spiti

The district gazetteer[4] of Lahaul and Spiti gives the population of the area, according to the 1961 census, as slightly more than twenty thousand. A little less than half of this population is Hindu. The Buddhist population is equally large. The rest of the population comprises Muslims. The terrain is mountainous. The atmosphere is bleak for the best part of the year; the rocky mountains are rugged and awe-inspiring; the land is criss-crossed by swift torrents that issue from glaciers. No wonder that the minds of the people are dominated by fear, and they are only too ready to seek protection from the mountain gods and other spirits they believe in. It is stated that in ancient days, prior to the advent of Buddhism, the people used to follow an animistic creed in which animals were sacrificed to appease evil spirits. In spite of the introduction of Buddhism, which does not tolerate any violence, goats and sheep are still sacrificed on such occasions as the opening of water courses and the beginning of the harvesting sesaon. In view of the severity of the weather, yaks are allowed to be killed even in areas where Buddhism is predominant.

The Western Himalaya came under the influence of Buddhism in the reign of Aśoka the Great in the third century B.C. Buddhism, however, caught the imagination

4. M.D. Mamgain, ed., Himachal Pradesh District Gazetters: Lahaul and Spiti (Chandigarh, 1975), pp. 51-66.

of the people in the eighth century A.D., when Guru Padmasambhava, a specialist in Buddhist *tantric* practices, visited the area. Since then Buddhism has played a great role in the life of the people. It is representesd today by the presence of a number of sects and their monastic orders. One can see the impact of Padmasmbhava's Lamaism all over the place. The Lamaism of Spiti interprets the Buddhist religion in its own unique way; so much so that purists feel that it is contaminated by local legends and superstitions and by the indigenous demonolatry of the region.

The people believe that there are many benevolent spirits and malevolent demons dwelling in the trees and the rocks. The Spiti Buddhists sacrifice goats and sheep to them in times of crisis or while seeking favours. They also believe in witches and sorceres and in the so-called evil eye. They cling to such beliets even today and pursue a rontine course of conduct for fear that any departure from it might bring down upon them dire punishment from the world of spirits. There is a taboo even on the planting of trees and on the opening of new sources of irrigation, as also on the use of old water ducts. (It would appear that they are afraid of annoying the *Klu*, the *Bon* deity of the nether world.)

The people of Lahaul observe certain ceremonies of a religious nature in connexion with the cultivation of their fields. A lama names a certain day as auspicious for commencing the ploughing of fields. Generally this day falls between the eighth and twenty second of May every year. After the fields have been ploughed and sown, a procession goes round the fields, preceded by one or two lamas and two drummers. Some people in this procession carry eiligious books on their backs. Then a feast is held with cakes and a kind of drink called *chang* supplied jointly by all the land holders. The object is to ensure better sprouting of the seeds sown. If the water courses for irrigating the fields need to be repaired, a sheep is offered by way of sacrifice to *lHa* who, the people believe, is the deity taking special care of the water courses. As soon as the seeds sprout, small branches of pencil ceder are planted at different places and subsquently burnt as incense. Meanwhile members of the family in each hut sit down, eat, and drink, and mumrur prayers. This is to ensure that the sprouted plants would grow vigorously and yield a larger quantity of grain. When the fields are nearing the ripening stage, a goat or sheep is sacrificed in honour of *lHa*. Simultaneously, horse races are held in several villages. Till this Festival of the Ripening Grain has been celebrated, nobody may cut grass or anything green with an iron sickle lest the god get angry and send frost to damage the harvest or even to destroy it. If anybody wants to cut grass before the festival, he may do so only with a sickle made of an ox horn or a sheep-horn or use his own hands. Any contravention of this rule would bring down severe punishment, normally in the form of fine. Money accumulated by levying the fine is used for buying chang for the village council.

Apart from eighteen well-known Buddhist monasteries and numerous chapels and shrines in private houses, some villages contain small temples dedicated to demons. Such temples are called *lHa khang*. They are unpretentious externally: they look like small, one-roomed houses though furnished inside much in the same manner as a private chapel. One or two fields are set apart in each village for the maintenance of such temples. Shrines found on hill-tops or in fields in the shape of niches cut in rocks on the sides of large masonary pillars are even less pretentious. They contain small images, each with a brass vessal for burning oil in front of it. Occasionally a lama comes and chants prayers before it. The belief in spirits and demons, the existence of *lHa khang* etc. suggest the widespread influence of *Bon* beliefs and practices. In fact, as the gazetteer states, Hinduism as practised in Lahaul is highly coloured by *Bon*, as well as by occultism and mystic ritual. When Buddhism came, people gladly, though imperceptibly, accepted the soothing forces of the Buddhist pantheon.

In 1869-70 the then Assitant Commissioner of Kulu prepared an account of the Himalayan districts of Kulu, Lahaul and Spiti on the basis of the notes he had jotted down in his diary.[5] The dominant faith in the kulu district, according to him, was Hinduism, but it was not the religion of the orthodox. The common people worshipped serpents and trees. They divided their gods into *devas, devīs*, *ṛṣis munis, yogīs*, forest fairies, and *nāgas*. Some of the *devas* and *devīs* bore the names of well-known Hindu divinities. Others bore peculiar names given to them in the villages in which their temples were located. Most Kulu people acknowleged the power of demons. Although they all honoured the well-known gods of the Hindu pantheon and paid reverence to them, they had a special affection for their own local deities. They invoked the help of those deities whenever they were in trouble, and they generally swore by them. At the time of festivals, when large numbers of people assembled, the priests worked themselves up into a frenzy by flogging themselves with steel chains and performed pantomimic actions with the sword or with fire and even acted as oracles.

5. A.F.P. Harcourt, The Himalayan Districts of Kooloo, Lahaul, and Spiti (Delhi, 1972), pp. 59-69.

There are a large number of temples dedicated to Hindu gods. Some of them suggest, by their shape and design, that Buddhism was once a widely followed religion in the region. Besides, there are shrines which suddenly come into view in some wooded recesses of the mountains or next to cascading mountain streams or in the midst of clusters of cedar trees. Theses are dedicated to the local deities. Sometimes such temples are made of only a few stones piled up anyhow to indicate the presence of the deities there.

And then there are temples built for the worship of the serpent gods. In these temples we find images made of wood. Sometimes iron casts of the likeness of a serpent are found screwed into the woodwork of doorposts. They are not just ornamental pieces without meaning. People in Kulu regard serpents as divine as long as they remain in tanks or under the stones of temples, but they do not hesitate to kill them if they come in their way. In some cases snakes are worshiped together with other divinities, but generally they receive exclusive worship.

Mention should also be made of tree worship. People drive nails into the trunk of a tree to get relief from pain. Shepherds offer weekly sacrifices before particular trees to ensure the safety and well-being of their flocks. In Lahaul the pencil cedar is especially adored. Certain bushes are regarded as sacred, and people consciously refrain from doing them injury.

The religon of the people of Lahaul is essentially Buddhism, with an admixture of Hinduism: it was never exclusively Buddhism. Prior to the advent of Buddhism there was a religion known as *Loong pai chos* (or the Religion of the valley) which consisted largely in the appeasement of spritis by sacrificing human beings.

Although Buddhism does not tolerate any shedding of blood, it has not so far been able to put an end to this from of worship. All that it has done is to persade people to sacrifice goats and sheep in the place of human beings.[6] It may, therefore, be said that there are three religions in Lahaul---*Loong pai chos*, Buddhism, and Hinduism. To a cartain extent the three religions are blended toghether. For instance, the people secretly eat cow's flesh or sacrifice a yak without any compunction, the sacrificial animal coming from a different house each time by rotation. As is well known, the killing of a cow is against the Hindu faith, and the Buddhists regard the taking of life itself as a sin. Each religion has its own peculiar beliefs which are respected by the other two. In the Hindu areas there are spots marked off as the abode of demons, and all are agreed that such spots should be treated with awe.

There are no separate shrines or temples for the worship of spirits in *Loong pai chos*. The people directly offer worship to the trees and rocks that they regard as sacred. *Loong pai chos* has numerous followers. In its ritul there is no role for Brahmins or lamas. It is not that this mysterious demon worship is confined only to low classes of people. The landlords share the superstitions of the common people, and to this day they worship idols which have no connexion with either Buddhism or Hinduism. There is a custom in Lahaul that grass should not be cut with anything but a wooden sickle or a sickle made out of horn till a certain auspicious day fixed for the purpose. On that day a goat is sacrificed and then, after the sacrifice has been made, the people are allowed to use iron tools and implements for cutting grass. So superstitious are the people who are not otherwise

6. Ibid.

unintelligent that any servant in their establishment found guilty of disobedience in the matter is most severely punished.

In Spiti, the religious faith is Buddhism, and it is purer here than in Lahaul. There is *Loong pai chos* too, but on a smaller scale.

A.H. Frencke once travelled from Shimla to the interior of the Himalayan region. He trekked along the left bank of the river Sutlej amd passed through Lahaul, Spiti, Kinnaur and Ladakh. He has recorded his experiences in a book entitiled *Antiquities of Indian Tibet*.

High up above Kalagtrung there is a locality called the Old Place of the Shar rgan Festival ("Shar rgan" means young and old). The chief event on the occasion of this festival in ancient times was human sacrifice. The festival as celebrated nowadays consists in the sacrifice of a goat. It is a kind of thanksgiving by parents who have been blessed with a son during the past year. The songs sung by people on this occasion remind one of the pre-Buddhist religion of Kanawar and Tibet. They refer to the religion of the people of the area as *lHa chos* and *Bon chos*. They not only speak of the deities of the *Bon* religion like *Gung sngon sngan lha* (the god of heaven). *sPang dmar lha* (the god of the red meadow), *Byar gọd* (the sun), etc. but alsc mention new deities like *Pho lha* and *Mo lha*. The god *Pho lha* and the goddess *Ṃo lha* stand for the creative principle. These are unmistakably the Tibetan names for *Śivā* and *Kālī*, the gods of the pre-Tibetan population of the Sutlej Valley. It is likely that human sacrifice, which was once a part of the *Shar rgan* festival, belonged to the religion of this aboriginal population and not to the Tibetans. (The Tibetans offered human sacrifice only at the time of affirming their loyaties

7. Ibid.

or at the conclusion of an important treaty or on the occasion of house-warming ceremony). *Śivā* and *Kālī* as found in the Himalaya are personifications of the creative power; they not only grant bountiful harvests but also bless people with children, especially sons. In fact people invoke the principal deities of the pre-Buddhist religion of Tibet, viz. *Kesar* and *'Brug gu ma* for the boon of children. This accountss for the affinity between the Tibetan pre-Buddhist religion and the aboriginal cult of *Śivā-Kālī* which one discerns in the *Shar rgan* hymns. *Kesar* and *'Brug gu ma* are not fierce like *Śivā* and *Kālī*. It would appear that *Śivā* and *Kālī* are regarded as propitious only when a part of what they have given is returned to them. Thus a portion of the harvest of the fields or some of the goats are returned to them through the sacrifice. They are also given some of the childern with whom they have blessed the village. This explains why human sacrifice is offered at the festival.

In Lhari, a village in Spiti, we can see the extensive ruins of an ancient castle called Serlang. Below the village there are many rock carvings, in particular of the ibex and the *swastika*. one of the carvings is the willow of the world with its six branches and six roots, one of the symbols of *Bon*. The ruins are thus ancient.

In the vicinity of the Tabo monastery too one can see ancient ruins and countless rock carvings. The carvings represnt mostly the ibex and the *swastika*. This shows that the place was once a flourishing centre of Bon.

There are five principal monasteries in Spiti. Three of them belong to the *dGe lugs pa* sect, the fourth to

---

8. A.H. Francke, Antiquities of Indian Tibet, Part I (New Delhi, n.d.), pp. 20-22.
9. Ibid., p.37.
10. Ibid., p.38.

the *Sa skya pa* sect, and the last to the *rNying ma pa* sect. The first four do not differ essentially from Central Tibetan establishments. In fact they are continually in touch with them. However, the Pyin monastery has nothing to do with Lhasa. It maintains its own ancient traditions. We have already seen the close connexion between the *rNying ma pa* sect with the preBudhist *Bon* religion (Chapter IV). Francke considers the Pyin monastery of Spiti a particularly suitable place for a study of this connexion.

Kinnaur

The district gazetteer says that the population of the district according to the census of 1961 was approximately 41,000. Nearly 90 per cent of the people are Hindus. The rest are Buddhists and Sikhs.

The people of Kinnaur are highly superstitious like the hills people.They regard many of the hills, caves, mountains, etc. as the regular haunts of spirits and supernatural beings.Every village has its deity . The people try to be on the right side of the village deity at all times from fear or devotion. Then there are ghosts and spirits which are dreaded. The people feel that the horns of certain domestic and wild animals have a power of their own.They hang these horns at the door of their houses to ward off evil.

Ghosts and evil spirits are supposed to dwell in the primaeval forests of deodar and pine.*Bakhar shuna* is a ghost believed to live in dense forests or on hill-tops. In shape it resembles a goat and makes a bleating sound.It can change its shape and throw stones at its victims. A person affected by this ghost is sure to be taken ill. *Banshir* is believed to live in the trees. It too can change

11. Ibid., p.47.

its shape at will. It can appear as a huge man, as a monkey, or as a jackal and make a gteat noise to frighten its victim.It is. however, not considered to be harmful. Usually it is active in the night.If the tree in which it lives is cut down and the timber used in consructing a house, it starts haunting the house. *Ruksas* is the ghost of a man who has sinned greatly. It generally prefers to live at the confluence of two streams, or on a huge rock, or in a cave, or on a tree. It may accost a man at night or even at noon. it has a frightful appearance, with long teeth and nails, and, assuming a huge shape, wrestles with its victim. *Khunkch* is an evil sprit supposed to reside in certain houses. If a marrige is celebrated in a house which it haunts or cattle are bought from such a house, this evil spirit may also accompany the bride or the cattle to the new house to torment the members of the new family or the cattle of the new house. In the Baspa Valley evil spirits are generally supposed to haunt and overpower innocent young girls. Peculiar devices are used to ward them off. The middle fingers of both the hands of the affected girl are tied together with hair.Chillis are burnt over embers, and the girl is made to sit in the midst of the smoke. The girl is also repeatedly asked to disclose the identity of the spirit. Then the spirit speaks through her and answers questions. Strangely enough, the girl provides answers in Hindustani of which she has no knowledge. Sometimes a big loaf made of ash and covered with the leaves of a pumpkin is placed where four paths converge.[12]

All this takes us back to *Shamanism* or *Bon.*

12. M.D. Mamgain ed., Himachal Pradesh Distiict Gazetteers: Kinnaur (Chandigarh, 1971), pp. 66-87.

Ladakh

Ladakh is both strange and beautiful. It is called differently by different people---such as "Indian Tibet", "West Tibet", or "Little Tibet." There are books entitled "Kashmir and Ladakh"although Ladakh is a part of the Indian state of Jummu and Kashmir. The British explorer Alexander Cunningham calls it Lạdak or Kha ba chan; the Swedish explorer Sven Hadin calls it trans -Himalaya; and the indian artist F.M.Hussain calls it Moonland.[13]

In ancient times the land was peopled by Tibetan nomads who professed *Bon*. Later there came the first Indian Budhist missionaries who made their way into the area over the Potu la Pass.Their successors are the Mons, who can still be found in Ladakh and can easily be distinguished from the other Ladakhis by their appearance and by the "purity" of their religion. Next to settle in Ladakh were the Dards from Bru sha. These introduced their own form of Budhism. (Traces of it still survive in some villages.) In the ninth century A.D.. there was a clash between the demonolatry of the earliest inhabitants and Buddhism. In the fourteenth century Buddhism clearly gained the upper hand. but only after it had assimilated a good many elements of *Bon*,so that there emerged a sort of blend of the two religions. A number of attempts were made from Lhasa to persuade the Ladakhis to accept the "purest" form of Buddhism. The result was anothor blend. Eventually the Red and Yellow monks settled for peacefull coexistence, each sect preserving its own brand of Buddhism.[14]

---

13. Heinrich Harrer, Ladakh: Gods and Mortals behind the Himalayas (Innsbruck, 1980), p.12.
14. Ibid., p. 13.

Ladakh could be called the land of spirits and demons, of magic ritual to ward them off, and of witchcraft. The conflict between good and evil is unceasing. A man must be on his guard against the powers of evil every moment. One could see mystic signs drawn on the walls and roof in every house to protect the inmates against evil spirits. There is a large head of wild sheep with branching horns mounted above the front door on the main beam of a house in Leh and painted in various colours. Nothing would induce the owners of the house to sell it since for them it was a protection against all illnesses brought on by evil spirits. The Ladakhis resort to innumerable methods of protecting themselves against spirits and demons like painting the corners of their houses red. They invite the presence of good spirits by daubing the walls with white crescents. They feel that they are constantly at the mercy of supernatural powers. They do not doubt the existence of such powers even for a moment. They do not embark upon any new project or undertake any journey without the approval of their oracles. There is not a single element of Ladakhi life that is not "protected". Pieces of paper inscribed with magic formula, amulets, scrolls of soothsayers, dolls suspended from caves, tridents impaled on human skulls, and the like are all used to keep off malevolent spirits and[15] demons

According to Francke, the religion of the Tibatn part of the population of Ladakh was from time immemorial *Bon* but without its systematized or organized strutcure. It was contact with Buddhilm that persuaded the people of the advisability of systematizing *Bon* and adopting certain forms from Buddhism. Consequently lists or water spirits (*klu*) and other supernatural beings were

15. Ibid., pp 128-40

drawn up and monasteries founded. The most famous *Bon po* monastery of Ladakh is, according to popular tradition, the gYung drung monastery (now called Lamayuru). It is so named after the *swastika* (in Tibetan, *gYung drung*), one of the symbols of *Bon* as well as of Buddhism. In the folklore of the area we could still find a good deal of the unsystematized *Bon.* Francke has documeted this religious system as found in the folklore of the region under the name of *gLing chos*. The main features of this religion are as follows:

The world consists of three great realms. First, there is the land of the gods of heaven, which is of white colour. Then there is the land of men, or the earth---of red colour. The third is the land of water spirits, or the lower world---of blue colour. There is a king ruling in heaven. There is a king ruling in the nether world also. The greatest is the Earth Mother. There is a huge tree, the tree of the world, growing through all the three realms. It has its roots in the nether world, and its highest branches are in heaven. The king of heaven sent one of his sons to rule over the earth. It is around the story of the mission of the youngest son of the king of heaven on the earth that the national epic of Tibet in genral, and of West Tibet in particular, revolves.[16]

The epic differs from village to village, but there is a version which may be called the official version. Lamaism took hold of this famous topic, and a poem was composed in which the ancient pre-Buddhist religious system was reconciled with Buddhism. However, this version has not found favour with the people; for they prefer to listen to the village bard when he sings to them of ancient things.[17]

16. Francke, n. 2, pp.82-85.
17. Ibid., pp. 87-92.

In the Indus Valley near rGya, the first village of Ladakh on the road from Rubshu, there are a number of large graves. Each of these graves contains rooms furnished with boards of pure wood. A number of skulls are placed on these boards. This points to the ancient custom of burying all the higher officials along with the dead body of the chief.[18]

Several miles from rGya there is the village Ubshi. A number of ancient *mchod rtens* may be seen around the village. Inside, the walls are covered with frescoes painted in indigo blue and brownish red. The frescoes show row upon row of figures of blue complexion, all seated cross-legged. The garments of these figures are white, with red seams. The head-dress is somewhat unusual. It looks as if the ends of a long hair-pin were projected on each side. These pictures appear to represent *nāgas (Klu);* the ancient *mchod rtens* are, clearly, *Bon po* structures.[19]

On a rock between Kargil and Chainigund in the Dard District, there are several rock carvings which remind us of the pre- Buddhist religion of Tibet. These carvings include especially a *swastika* and a *yoni* and several ibex. At a place called Dong ga there is a boulder which also has many carvings. The older ones are of a yellowish colour, the more recent ones are white. Most of the more recent carvings represent ibex, but there are no scenes of ibex-hunting. The ibex is a symbol of fertility in the pre-Buddhist religion. Deities like *Kesar* and *'Bru gu* ma are invoked to obtain children. When a child is born, the neighbours make presents of ibex made of flour to the happy family. The numerous figures of the ibex

18. Francke, n. 8, p.65.
19. Ibid., p. 66.

carved on the rocks of Ladakh thus represent thanks offerings for the birth of children. The custom appears to be still in vogue if we go by the carvings of the ibex. (These carvings are white in colour.)[20]

Tradition says that the monastery of Lamayuru was once the centre of the *Bỏn* religion in Ladakh.[21] It was called *gYung drung*. It received its name from the sprouting and growing of sacrificial grain in the shape of the *swastika*. This monastery was a well-known centre of learning even before Na ro pa arrived in Ladakh (in the ninth or the tenth century). It was in fact a place of primary importance. It was later converted into a Buddhist monastery and named Lamayuru.

Below the monastery there is an ancient shrine which appears to be an old *Bon po* temple. All the divinities painted on the walls of the hall of the temple are of the Buddhist type, but their complexion is either blue or black, and their dress is red. These pictures seem to represent *nāgas* similar to the ones to be found at Ubshi and Alchi. All this suggests that the temple is one of *Bon po* origin, but erected during the period when the *Bon* religion was largely under the influedce of Hinduism and Buddhism. None of the Buddha-shaped figures preserved in the temple is of white, yellow, or red complexion.[22]

Besides, there are frescoes in which priests of the *Bon* religion are repesented. One of them is almost life-size; others are smaller. They are all clothed in white undergarments and striped gowns. The stripes on the gown of the large figure and on that of one of the smaller ones

20. Ibid., p. 96.
21. Ibid.
22. Ibid., p. 97.

are black and blue, the stripes on the gowns of the others are black and grey. The large figure is wearing a blue hat, the small figures have hats of the same shape but of black colour. The early references to the dress of *Bon po* priests describe it as either black or blue. According to Francke, these relics of the *Bon* religion at Lamayuru are of some importance; for the present-day *Bon po* priests of Central Tibet cannot be distinguished fron the Buddhist in view of the similarity of the dress.[23]

Snellgrove and sKorupsky[24] do not agree with Francke. They say that when they visited Ladakh in 1974-75, they found no ancient shrine of the kind Francke identifies as an ancient *Bon po* temple at Lamayuru. They, of course, add that an acquaintance of theirs, on a visit to Ladakh in 1971, had seen an old temple being knocked down by the villagers. They feel that Francke has based his conclusion on false information given to him locally. As for the colour of the garments of the figures, they contend that Kashmiri Buddhist teachers "as portrayed at Alchi" also wear similar striped garments. There too, they point out, the five Buddhas on Maitreya's crown are all invested with blue garments—with garments in a colour Which Francke seems to regard "quite wrongly as exclusively *Bon*". Again they feel that the paintings photographed by Francke and identified as *Bon po* are more likely to be of Indian Buddhist teachers in the style preserved better at Alchi. According to them Francke

> ...seems to confuse *Bon* in its more popular meaning of pre-Buddhist religion and its more accurate meaning as referring to an unusual Tibetan Buddhist sect, which deliberately combined Buddhist teachings with other extraneous as well as indigenous beliefs and whose members from at least the 13th century onwards built

---

23. Ibid., p. 98.
24. David L. Snellgrove and Tadeusz sKorupsky, The Culutal Heritage of Ladakh (New Delhi, 1977), vol. 1, p. 21.

temples in Buddhist imitation. There is no sign of this sect ever spreading to Ladakh.[25]

Zanskar

Michel Peissel, French anthropologist and explorer, succeeded in scaling the formidable mounatain range that has preserved the title of Zanskar and in visting the middle Himalayan kingdom in 1976. He traversed the whole land, visited various monasteries, stayed in the houses of inhabitants, and wrote a book in which he has given a detailed account of the region and its people. The book was published in 1979.

It is a general belief in Zanskar that the Amdo region, which is a good 3,800 miles from there and is twenty times its size and has a population twenty times as large, was originally inhabited by people fron Zanskar. Many young monks used to go there to study. (Amdo incidentally is a stronghold of the *Bon po.*) This is rather surprising because the journey itself took a year and a half of continuous walking. So strong is the belief that they have a legend about it. This legend relates how a young man from Zanskar went to Amdo and found a vast lake (Lake Kokonor.) Out of this lake there emerged a beautiful princess. The two fell in love and had many children. This is how, according to them, the people of Amdo have the same bones (or blood) as the inhabitants of Zanskar. Whatever the truth, the connexion between Amdo and Zanskar is remarkable if not improbable. During his travels Peissel himself met many monks who had spent several years in Amdo and who showed him printed banners attesting to the strong links between the two regions.[26]

25. Ibid.
26. Michel Peissel, Zanskar. The Hidden Kingdom (New York, 1979), pp. 54-55.

All the four sects of Tibetan Buddhism are to be found in Zanskar. The oldest is the rNying ma pa sect. Those who belong to this sect believe not only in classical Buddhist texts but also in the revealed texts. They have incorporated many magical practices in their ritual that can be traced to the *Bon* religion which once dominated Central Asia. In the other Buddhist sects of the area there are hordes of hideous and evil-looking spirits. According to Peissel, these are imported from the Hindu pantheon along with countless magical rites and supersitions of the ancient *Bon* religion of Central Asia.[27]

Peissel says that in the Kargya Valley of Zanskar there is a grassy pasture on which there is a stone throne. The throne is covered with little piles of white stones. It is an altar; the white stones are offerings made to the divinity who is believed to live in the cliff. The altar throne is located at the foot of the cliff. Around, there are several such cliffside shrines or altars surrounded by low cairns, stones stacked one on top of another, and piles of pebbles set up in honour of the mysterious *lu* (*Klu*), the little known pre-Buddhist *Bon* divinity of the Himalaya. Most *Bon* divinities are believed to inhabit water, rocks, earth, and mountain peaks; others live inside unusual rocks or cliff formations. Peissel says that many Buddhist shrines and monasteries are places that have been converted from those meant for the worship of the elusive *lu* of old. The Lunak province is especially the land of black spirits. It is a primitive, isolated region which is the home of archaic beliefs.[28]

27. Ibid.
28. Ibid., pp. 181-2.

Select Bibliography

Aziz, Barbara Nimri, and Matthew Kapstein, eds, Soundings in Tibetan Civilization (New Delhi: manohar Publications, 1985).

Bapat, P.V. 2500 Years of Buddhism (New Delhi: Goverenment of India, Ministry of Information and Broadcasting, Publications Division, 1987).

Barua, Benimadho, A History of Pre-Buddhist Indian Philosophy (Delhi : Matilal Banarsidass, 1981).

Bechert, Heinze, and Richard Gombrich, eds, The World of Buddhism (Lodon: Thomas and Hudson, 1984).

Bell, Sir Charles, The people of Tibet (Oxford: Clarendon Press, 1928).

. . . . . , The Religions of Tibet (Oxford: Clarendon Press, 1931)

Dass, Sarat Chandra, Contributions on Religious History of Tibet (New Delhi: Manjushri publishing House, 1970).

Denwood, Phillips, and Platogorsky, eds, Buddihist Studies, Ancient and Modren (London: university of London, School of Oriental and African Studies, 1982).

Dhargyey, Ngawang, "The Kalachakra Initiation," Tibet Journal (Dharamsala), vol. 1, no. 1, 1975.

Ekval, Robert B., Tibetan Skylines (new York: Ferrar Strauss and Young, 1952).

-----, "Singnificance of Thirteen as a Symbolic Number in Tibetan and mongolian Cultures", Journal of American Oriental Society (New Haven, Conn.), no. 3, 1956.

-----, Religious Obervances in Tibet (Chicago, III.: University of Chicago Press, 1964).

-----, The Lama Knows (New Delhi: Oxford and IBH Publishing Company, 1979).

Evans-Wentz, W.Y. ed., The Tibetan Book of Great Liberation (London:Oxford University Press, 1967).

Fatone, Vicente, Philosophy of Nagarjūnā (Delhi: Motilal Banarisdass, 1981).

Fisher, James F., ed., Himalayan Anthropology: The Indo-Tibetan Interface (The Hague: Mouton, 1978).

Francke, A. H., A History of Western Tibet (New Delhi: Sterling Publishers, 1977).

-----, Antiquities of Indian Tibet, Vol. I.(Delhi: S Chand and Company, n.d.)

Govinda, Lama Anagarika, The way of the White Clouds (Bombay: B. I. Publications 1982).

Haas, Ernst, and Minke, Gisela, " The Kalachakra Initiation", Tibet Journal, vol. 1, nos 3-4, autumn 1976.

Harcourt, A.F.P., The Himalayan Districts of Kooloo, Lahaul and Spiti (Delhi: Vivek Publishing House, 1972).

Harrer, Heinrich, Ladakh: Gods and Mortals behind the Himalayas (Innsbruck: Penguin Verlag, 1980).

Hiriyana, M., An Outline of Indian Philosophy (London: George Allen and Unwin, 1967).

Hoffman, Helmut, The Religions of Tibet, Edward Fitzgerald, trans (London: George Allen and Unwin, 1962).

Joshi, L. M. Discerning Buddha (Delhi: Munshiram Manoharlal, 1983).

Kaloyanov, Stanimir, "Inrano-Tibetica: Some Observations on Bon," Tibet Journal, vol. 15, no. 1, spring 1990.

Karmay, Samten G., ed., A Treasury of Good Sayings: A Tibetan history of Bon (London: Oxford University Press, 1972).

-----, A General Introduction to the History and Doctrines of Bon (Tokyo: Toyo Bunko, 1975).

Kuznetsov, B.I., "Who Was the Founder of Bon Religion?, Tibet Journal, vol. 1, no. 1, spring 1975.

Lhalungpa, Lobsang, "The Religious Culture of Tibet", ibid, vol. 1, no. 3, autumn 1976.

Liyu Yi, "Tibetology: A Chinese View." ibid., vol. 8, no. 2, summer 1983.

Mamgain, M.D., ed., Himachal Pradesh District Gazetteers: Lahaul and Spiti (Chandigarh: Government of Himachal Pradesh, 1975).

-----, Kinnaur (Chandigarh: Government of Himachal Pradesh, 1971).

Nebesky-Wijkowitz, Rene De, The Oracles and Demons of Tibet (The Hague: Mouton, 1956).

Norbu, Namkhai, "Bon and Bonpos" Tibetan Review (New Delhi), December 1980.

-----, The Nacklace of GZI: A Cultural History of Tibet (Dharamsala: Information Office of His Holiness The Dalai Lama, 1981).

Norbu, Thubten Jigme, and Colin M. Turnbull, Tibet: Its History, Religion, and People (London: Chatto and Windus, 1969).

Peissel, Michel, Zanskar: The Hidden kingdom (New York: E.P. Dutton, 1979).

Per Kvaerne, "The Canon of Tibetan Bonpos" Indo-Iranian journal (Boston, Mass), no. 16, 1975.

----, "The Genesis of Tibetan Buddhist Tradition." Tibetan Review, March 1976.

-----, "A Set of Thangkas Illustrating the Life of sTon-pa gShen-rab", Tibet journal, vol. 12, no. 3, autumn 1987.

Richardson, Hugh, "Ministers of Tibetan kingdom", Tibet Journal, vol. 2, no.1, spring 1977.

Rock, J.F., The Nakhi Naga Cult and Related Ceremonies, Part I (Roma: Is M.E.O, 1952).

Rockhill, W.Woodwill, The Life of Buddha (Varanasi: Orientala India, 1972.)

Shakabpa, W. D. Tsepon, Tibet: A Political History (New Haven, Conn./London: Yale University press, 1967).

sKorupsky, Tadeusz, "Tibetan gYung-drung Monastery at Dolanji", Kailash (Kathmandu), vol. 8, nos 1-2, 1981.

Smart, John, and John Wehrheim, "Dolpo, Nepal", Tibet Journal, vol. 2, no, 1, spring 1977.

Snellgrove, Daviod L. The Buddhist Himalaya (Oxford: Bruno Cassier, 1957).

-----, Four Lamas of Dolpo (Oxford: Bruno Cassier, 1967).

-----, Nine Ways of Bon (Boulder, colo.: Prajna Press, 1980).

-----, Himalayan Pilgrimage (Boulder, Colo.: Prajna Press, 1981).

-----, and Hugh E. Richardson, A Cultural history of Tibet (Boulder, Colo.: Prajna Press, 1980).

Snellgrove, David L., and Tadeusz sKorupsky, The Cultural Heritage of Ladakh, Vol. I (New Delhi: Vikas Publishing House, 1977).

Stein, R.A. Tibetan Civilisation (London: Faber and Faber, 1962.)

Swami Pranavananda, Kailash Mansarovar (Calcutta: S.P.League, 1949).

Thomas, J. Edward, The Life of the Buddha as Legend and history (London: Routledge and Kegan Paul, 1927).

Tucci, Giuseppe, To Lhasa and Beyond (Rome: Institute Poligrafico del stat, 1956).

-----, The Religions of Tibet (New Delhi: Allied Publishers, 1980).

Uray, G., The Old Tibetan Word Bon (Budapest: Acta orientalia, 1964), tomus 17, fasc 3.

Waddel Austin L., The Buddhism of Tibet or Lamaism (London: W. H. Allen and Company, 1895).

Winternitz Maurice, A History of indian Literature (Delhi: Bharatiya Vidya Prakashan, 1987).

INDEX

D

L

M

N

T